# Your
# School
*of* Love

# Your
# School
## *of* Love

*A Spiritual Companion*
*for Homeschooling Mothers*

**AGNES M. PENNY**

TAN Books
Charlotte, North Carolina

Cataloging-in-Publication data on file with the Library of Congress.

Cover design by Caroline Kiser

Cover image ©iStockphoto.com/kupicoo

ISBN: 978-1-61890-212-2

Published in the United States by
Saint Benedict Press, LLC
PO Box 410487
Charlotte, NC 28241
www.SaintBenedictPress.com

Printed and bound in the United States of America.

TAN Books
Charlotte, North Carolina
www.TANBooks.com
2014

# CONTENTS

v

# AUTHOR'S NOTE

THIS is not a how-to-homeschool book. Nor is this a how-I-homeschool book. Rather, this is a spiritual companion for homeschooling mothers or fathers, both beginners and veterans, meant to refresh, inspire, and offer practical suggestions for those who dare to take charge of their children's education.

Truth never changes and is the same for everyone, but not everyone will use the same method for communicating this truth. People have different personalities, learning styles, interests, and needs, and thus different families will find that different educational styles work best for them. As homeschooling parents, we shouldn't assume the educational method that was used to teach us, or methods we've seen others use, are necessarily the methods best suited for ourselves and our children. I hope this book helps homeschoolers to discover the best methods for their unique families. To that end, I've made a lot of suggestions in the following pages, not intending the reader to follow them all, but hoping that if one suggestion doesn't work for one family, another suggestion will. My goal is to encourage homeschoolers to try a more relaxed, more natural, less stressful style of learning. This will look different in different homes, and will probably change in each home as the children grow and their needs and interests change. While this relaxed attitude towards education will be applied differently in different homes, it should diminish burnout and discipline struggles wherever it is adopted, and provide a fun, unstressful learning experience for the whole family.

Not every meditation in this book will apply exclusively to homeschoolers. After all, homeschooling is just an extension of parenthood, requiring all the same virtues and habits and attitudes of good parenting—only more so, because homeschoolers spend more time and do a greater variety of activities with their children than non-homeschooling parents. Some chapters will talk about topics like how to cultivate humility in ourselves or encourage creativity in our children—issues equally applicable to homeschoolers and non-homeschoolers. Similarly, some chapters, like "Homeschooling a Large Family," may contain some tips that could help both large and small homeschooling families. Each meditation is preceded by a quote from a well-known Catholic—often a saint—which can help us keep perspective in our daily battle against cluttered rooms, soiled laundry, and misplaced modifiers.

Most of the books and resources I recommend in this book are ones I've personally read or used; however, I did include a few that I have not read because I wanted to provide a variety of suggestions not limited to those I've had the time or money to actually look over myself. However, either my children or I have read the majority of the books mentioned, and I feel confident recommending them to homeschooling families. I encourage readers to look up book suggestions online and to look over online reviews or even read a few sample pages before making a purchase. Many of the books mentioned are no longer in print, but I did not want to limit the selection to books which happened to be published recently, particularly since finding used books has become easier than ever before with used book websites, where the treasures of the past can be rediscovered and cherished by families of today.

Taking responsibility for a child's education is a huge and daunting task, sometimes frustrating and bewildering, often exhausting, but always rewarding. I hope to affirm you in your choice to educate your child at home and to assist you with spiritual reflections that have helped me in the daily grind of managing parenthood, discipline, laundry, cooking, cleaning, and—oh, yes—overseeing the academic and intellectual formation of my children. I pray that God will bless you in your efforts to raise cultured, literate, and virtuous children, and that my book might assist you a little bit in your journey.

*"It is necessary not only that religious instruction be given to the young at certain fixed times, but also that every other subject taught, be permeated with Christian piety. If this is wanting, if this sacred atmosphere does not pervade and warm the hearts of masters and scholars alike, little good can be expected from any kind of learning, and considerable harm will often be the consequence."*

—PIUS XI, ON CHRISTIAN EDUCATION

# 1

# HOMESCHOOLING

*"The parents have been appointed
by God Himself as the first and
principal educators of their children . . .
their right is completely inalienable."*

—POPE JOHN PAUL II

HOMESCHOOLING is what we make it. That's why it is such an adventure. We decide just what our homeschool will look like. We determine the environment in which our children will discover the wonders of the universe that God has created, the amazing stories of the heroic men and women who have lived before us, the fascinating world of numbers and shapes, and the classic tales that the great minds of our civilization have written. We choose what books and resources to use, what atmosphere will pervade our home, and what crafts, games, artwork, and music will lighten the day's load. We design our daily schedule, along with beloved family traditions, whether we read the life of the saint of the day aloud at breakfast, recite the Angelus at lunch, sing songs together in the car while doing errands, or pray the rosary as a family before bed.

Homeschooling is what we make it. We can imitate the conventional school system, buy a chalkboard, maps, textbooks, and workbooks, and keep our children busy all day with paperwork. Or we can follow the revolutionary lead of unschoolers and let our children initiate all their own learning experiences. Or, like most homeschoolers, we can choose a path somewhere in between, more or less rigid, more or less relaxed, more or less hands-on in our approach. It's up to us. We should take the time to learn about different educational methods to help us determine what approach we want to adopt. Our choice will depend on our own temperament and learning style, the temperaments and learning styles of our children, as well as the time and resources at our disposal. Most of us have experienced conventional schooling at great length; to attain a more balanced perspective, we need to give some consideration to the ideas of Charlotte Mason, John Holt, John Taylor Gatto, Raymond Moore, Mary Hood, Rick and Marilyn Boyer, Suzie Andres, and others. Whether we agree with these educators or not, we can learn both from our agreements and from our disagreements as we grope towards our own educational philosophy.

Homeschooling is what we make it. Homeschooling can be exciting or boring, fun or tedious, inspiring or discouraging. We can feel weighed down by the tremendous responsibility and complain about the enormous amount of work we have ahead of us, or we can treasure this precious time we have to spend with our children, exulting in the opportunity to be with our children as they first count to ten, sound out their first word, look through their first microscope, speak their first sentence in French, gasp over *Treasure Island*, and cry over *Little Women*.

Homeschooling is what we make it. We can thank God for the unique advantages homeschooling affords our family: precious time spent together, shelter from the materialism and impurity of the world, and the ability to make our faith a part of every moment of our day. We can thank Him for the flexibility of homeschooling which allows us to accommodate the needs of each child, going slower where he needs extra work and advancing more quickly in subjects he finds easy. We can thank Him for the opportunity to focus on the interests of each child, choosing books that pique each one's curiosity and adapting our teachings style to each one's learning style. Those of us with children who have learning disabilities have special reasons to thank God for this flexibility, but all homeschooling parents will thrill to the sight of their child thriving in an environment where his intellectual interests, strengths, and weaknesses determine the curricula.

Homeschooling is what we make it. If we see it as a burden, it will be a burden. If we see it as a joy, it will be a joy. If we see it as a grave but rewarding responsibility, a vocation within a vocation, then that's what it will be. If we see homeschooling as an opportunity to mold the intellectual, cultural, and spiritual character of our children, and our own personal path to grow closer to our children and to Christ, then it will be that, as well.

# 2

# WHY HOMESCHOOL?

*"It has been discovered that with a dull urban
population, all formed under a mechanical
system of State education, a suggestion or
command, however senseless and unreasoned,
will be obeyed if it be sufficiently repeated."*

—HILAIRE BELLOC

MANY homeschoolers begin homeschooling for one
reason, but find so many benefits in it that they
continue to homeschool for completely different reasons.
Before we begin our reflections on homeschooling, let's
consider some of the reasons why we homeschool, and this
will help us to form our own homeschool according to our
ideals.

Here are some reasons why many of us homeschool:

1. We do not trust the public or parochial schools
   not to expose our children to inappropriate
   movies and books, sex education classes, or
   politically correct propaganda.

5

2. We do not trust the other students in the local schools not to introduce our children to impure jokes, bad language, etc.

3. We do not want our children to grow up with an inordinate desire for name brand clothes, popular music, television shows, and various inappropriate toys that are given to children in our society.

4. We do not want our children to develop a low self-esteem, lack of confidence, or poor social skills because of the ridicule and ostracism they may experience at school when we do not allow them to have or do what the other students have or do.

5. We do not want our children to be like sheep, following everyone else's ideas on style, music, books, politics, etc., because of peer pressure. On the contrary, we want our children to be independent thinkers, with critical and analytical minds, capable of forming their own reasonable opinions.

6. Homeschoolers are able to adapt the lessons according to the needs of each child, going over difficult material again in different ways until he comprehends it and moving more quickly over material our child finds easy so he will not become bored.

7. Homeschooling takes only a fraction of the time that classroom schooling takes, leaving hours free for unstructured play, which builds children's imaginations, strengthens their social skills and their ability to communicate, and allows them a safe way to explore the consequences of different choices. This is truly the optimal time for learning for children. Their interest is fully engaged, and they are free to combine skills they've learned separately during lessons, and to experiment with and explore all sorts of ideas that they have picked up throughout the day.

8. Homeschooling also leaves plenty of time for unassigned reading, which not only imparts new ideas and information, but also builds vocabulary, spelling, and grammar skills, and superior writing styles.

9. Again, homeschoolers have more time for hobbies and crafts, which help children develop creativity, problem-solving skills, and confidence as they complete projects.

10. Some of a homeschooling student's free time can also be devoted to household chores, which cultivate responsibility, teach innumerable skills that children will use in their adult life, and also build confidence as they

realize they are contributing to the family's well-being in a meaningful way. Moreover, having this help can make a world of difference to a mother of a large family, enabling her to be more cheerful and patient through the day and to spend more individual time with each child.

11. We have one or more boys. Boys' brains work very differently from girls', and since most school systems are dominated by women, often boys will find themselves at a disadvantage in a classroom setting unwittingly designed for the learning style of the female mind. (Granted, in most homeschooling families the mothers teach the boys; nevertheless, by teaching one-on-one, a mother can better accommodate each child's unique learning style, masculine or feminine, than can a teacher dealing with a class of twenty or more students.) Furthermore, research shows that boys are not ready for a structured environment at the same age as girls, and even when they are ready, sitting still during the greater part of the day is simply an unnatural requirement for active boys, which can easily lead to apathy for all things academic.

12. We want to eliminate much of the tedium of school for our girls. Homeschooling allows children—boys and girls—to spend only

a short time on formal lessons in their own home, and much of that time can be spent in enjoyable activities, such as reading history books out loud to their siblings or playing math games together. When lessons are interesting, the children will retain their love of learning and they'll remember what they learn better. For example, because homeschooled children are not tired of sitting and doing paperwork all day, they often write stories without being told to, just for fun. Moreover, because their motivation is not to complete an assignment, but to please themselves and each other, they try harder to produce a good story.

13. We have one or more children with special needs. Children with special needs, from ADHD to dyslexia, from autism to Downs' Syndrome, tend to thrive in an environment where they receive one-on-one attention from their teacher and are not distracted by the unfamiliar sights and sounds around them. Homeschooling these children allows us to give them the individual attention they need, to provide an environment that helps them focus on their lessons, and to adapt the curricula to suit their particular strengths and weaknesses.

14. Our children would miss a lot of school days if in conventional schools, perhaps because the

family travels or moves frequently, or because of health issues, or because of a focused commitment to an extracurricular activity like dance, music, or sports. Homeschooling allows the flexibility of learning in the car, on a train, or even in bed.

15.   Homeschooled children tend to do better academically than their peers. While this may not be our primary motivation to homeschool—in fact, many Catholic mothers would sacrifice some academic quality of education to ensure the spiritual and emotional wellbeing of their children—still, academic excellence is a strong encouragement to continue homeschooling.

16.   Homeschooling strengthens family unity. Our children's best friends are each other. Rather than sneering at the idea of playing with a younger sibling, they enjoy playing together; furthermore, they learn to work with each other's strengths and weaknesses and to help those younger than themselves. Their interests are centered around family events, like birthdays, feast days, a baby getting a new tooth or an older child losing a tooth, rather than keeping up with trendy clothes or who has a crush on whom.

17.   We love spending time with our children.

Not everyone homeschools for all of these reasons. However, being aware of many of the possible reasons for homeschooling can help us reap the benefits of homeschooling in our own homes.

In future chapters we will explore some of these benefits at greater length. Right now, let us reflect on the incredible flexibility and numerous advantages that homeschooling provides, and thank God for the opportunity He has so graciously given us to spend this precious time raising, forming, and loving our children. Let us see homeschooling, not as a burden, but as a blessing replete with more rewards than we have yet realized.

# 3

# THE VOCATION TO
# HOMESCHOOL

*"To fall in love with God is the
greatest of all romances; To seek Him,
the greatest adventure; To find Him,
the greatest human achievement."*

—ST. AUGUSTINE

WHATEVER our situation, whatever trials or
unique circumstances face us, we have chosen to
homeschool our children because we strongly feel that this
is the best thing we can possibly do for them. What we
must also realize is that if God is calling us to homeschool
our children, then homeschooling must be what is best
for us, as well. It is a vocation within a vocation, our own
particular path to holiness, our way to cultivate a deeper
relationship with Christ. Like St. Martha, busy with many
things, bogged down by a thousand little details, we must
nevertheless use this vocation as a means to grow closer to
Our Lord, for that is why He gave it to us. Our spiritual life
cannot be put on the back burner until our youngest child

finishes high school. Not only would that mean failing to give our children the example they need, it would also mean throwing away the wonderful opportunity God has given us, here and now, to grow in sanctity.

Of course, we may not have as much time to pray as we used to, and certainly not as much as we would like to have. Still, we must make some time for prayer. Interrupted prayer is still prayer. Dealing with the interruptions patiently is also a prayer. In fact, as the day progresses, our mental prayer will naturally give way to active prayer as we bustle through the house, preparing meals, singing songs, answering questions, reading a loud, digging up materials for a science experiment, folding laundry, and performing all the little acts of love we do each day. Everything we do becomes an act of love, a prayer to Our Lord, an offering of our hearts.

Homeschooling makes huge demands on our time, our energy, our patience, and our emotions. These are the gifts we present to God. We give Him everything we have and everything we do. We mustn't be afraid or upset because our gifts to God are not perfect; nor should we imagine that we are the only homeschooling mother who ever makes mistakes, who ever snaps or shouts at her children, who ever makes an imprudent decision. No. We are all sinners; all of us are fallible. We misjudge situations, make unfair decisions, lose our tempers, discipline inconsistently, and give a bad example to our children. As one homeschooling father said, "If you're not throwing interceptions, you're not playing quarterback." We all make mistakes; we all sin; and we all feel humbled at our unworthiness.

But to dwell on our sinfulness to the point of discouragement or self-disparagement is not only fruitless, it's destructive and dangerous. We must embrace homeschooling as our own personal path toward growing more patient, more loving, more humble, more forgiving, more self-sacrificing, more self-disciplined, more industrious, more prudent, and more saintly. We must see homeschooling as our way to perfect ourselves and grow closer to Christ.

In this sense, our homeschool becomes our own personal school of love—not only a school where we teach, but a school where we learn—a school where we learn about and meditate on the enormity of Christ's love for us, and where we fall in love with Christ and learn to love Him in every thought, word, and deed. For only if we are truly caught up in the wonder and joy of Christ's love for us, as demonstrated most obviously on the cross and in the tabernacle, and only if we are completely enraptured and absorbed in His infinitely loving and generous heart, can we really share in His love and show that love to our children. Then we can rejoice that God has called us to this vocation within a vocation, and we can truly call our home a school of love.

# 4

## BURNOUT

*"We are not drawn to God by iron chains, but
by sweet attractions and holy inspirations."*

—ST. FRANCIS DE SALES

PERHAPS our biggest enemy in our vocation as homeschoolers is burnout. We work so hard to get everything done, to teach enthusiastically, to coordinate lessons, to keep on top of housework, to plan projects, to grade tests, and then we suddenly hit our limit and we can't go on any longer. We struggle to keep going, but in the process we become cranky, impatient, and discouraged, and the smallest annoyances or tasks become unbearably trying.

What went wrong? Could it be that perhaps our vision of homeschooling is just a little askew? Have we designed a homeschool that no real woman could ever manage on a long-term basis while also running a household? Is there another way of homeschooling our children, a way that we can educate our children without neglecting housework and still keep our sanity, our peace, and our joy? Is there a way we can homeschool and still have the time to pray and grow in holiness without becoming overwhelmed by all our responsibilities?

The answer is yes. Homeschooling is what we make it. We can approach our homeschool with a perfectionist attitude and dream of coordinating lessons, crafts, field trips and supplemental reading; we can pattern our own homeschool after the public or parochial schools that we attended, with all the ensuing busy work, papers, and tests that classroom teachers use; unfortunately, burnout will most likely result.

In fact, homeschooling does not have to be a public or parochial school in miniature. As Mary Hood points out in *The Joyful Homeschooler*, as homeschooling mothers, our role does not need to change from mother to teacher during part of the day. Our house does not need to become a classroom. On the contrary, homeschooling is merely an extension of our motherhood, another way to spend time and share experiences with our children. Yes, we teach our children, just as we have been teaching them since the time they were born. Yes, we provide academic rules and requirements, just as we've provided rules and requirements for them in every other aspect of life. We are not taking on a new role; we are just extending our role as mothers to yet another facet of our children's lives. Homeschooling simply allows us, as mothers, to spend more time with our children and to be involved in more of their daily activities—a privilege and opportunity few mothers today have.

When we look at homeschooling this way, we can breathe a deep sigh of relief, sit back, and relax. We can enjoy being with our children again. If we feel burnt out, we probably should try a period of de-schooling—a few weeks or even a month or two—during which we put aside all formal academic lessons. This will allow us and our children to disassociate the ideas of homeschooling and stress. When we feel relaxed and energetic again, we can gradually return to the task of educating our children, but without the pressure and perfectionism. The ideas in the following chapters are aimed at helping homeschooling parents to learn to teach their children without stress or pressure and to truly enjoy their time with them.

A cranky, discouraged, or stressed-out woman cannot effectively fulfill her duties as teacher or mother, and is certainly a poor sample of a saint, which is our ultimate goal. Therefore, we have to avoid burnout for own sake and for the sake of our children. Fortunately, there is a way to homeschool without getting stressed, overwhelmed, or burned out; a way in which we can enjoy educating our children, keep on top of the housework, and grow holier. But for all of this to take place, we have to make love the motivation in our homeschool, rather than fear or worry. We must put aside anxieties about "covering everything" or conforming to the school district or impressing our neighbors. We must begin to see our children, not as students with minds to be filled with certain information, but as people—precious, immortal souls—to be nurtured, taught, and loved. Their needs and their interests must take precedence over our preconceived lesson plans. Their questions must be answered, their feelings and learning styles respected, and their lessons filled with laughter and hugs. This is not to say that we will never require them to do academic work that is distasteful to them; however, true love respects and loves even while it teaches and disciplines; true love looks beyond the information presented in a lesson plan to the current needs of the student here and now; true love seeks not merely to teach but to educate, mold, and nurture; and this attitude will transform our homeschool into a school of love.

# 5

# A LEARNING ENVIRONMENT

*"Gentle love scatters abroad an aura*
*of joy and peace."*

—ST. JANE FRANCES DE CHANTAL

S O, how exactly do we approach homeschooling in a
way that avoids stress and burnout? Simply stated, we
must remember that our vocation has made us mothers,
not teachers; our household is made up of a family, not a
school. We don't need to spend all our energy coordinating curricula, grading papers, or motivating our children
to learn. We just need to create a learning environment in
our home, and our children will learn, whether we teach
them or not.

The most important factor in creating a learning environment is to eliminate the TV. The TV is probably the
biggest reason for the plummet in the level of education
in the last few decades, because children who watch a lot
of TV don't tend to read very much, and reading is what
trains young minds to think, to communicate, and to discover worlds and viewpoints beyond their own. We need

to regulate the TV to one or two hours a week, and if we can't stick to that, then we need to unplug it and throw it either in the attic or in the garbage can.

Equally counterproductive to a learning atmosphere is the influence of the Internet and other forms of technological entertainment, such as video games, iPhones, iPods, etc. There is hardly any reason why a child should need to use the Internet; if we are concerned about children keeping pace with technology in the real world, we shouldn't be; the Internet is so easy to use that a teenager could easily master the basics in one sitting. Moreover, by the time the child is old enough to need the Internet, the chances are strong that technology will have changed so much that much of what he learns now will be obsolete. However, if we do decide to allow our children to use the Internet, we should carefully limit the time; an hour or so a week should be sufficient. Of course, because immoral content on the Internet is so easy to access, we need to monitor our children while they are using the Internet, for example by keeping the computer in an open area of the house, rather than in a bedroom. Most school research should be done using encyclopedias or other books, rather than the web. Internet searches should be limited to activities that cannot be done any other way; perhaps looking up local concerts, volunteer opportunities, part-time jobs, book sales, or developing photos, etc. Our child's social life should not be centered on a webpage, chat room, or Facebook, but should involve real people whom they meet in real life. Some friends may insist that they can only set up a time to get together through email; but we must not let ourselves be pressured by the decisions of other families. We should allow our child to have an email account only if we *want* him to have one.

The main problem with the Internet is that it creates a simulated reality, completely divorced from the real world, centered only on the individual using it. It panders to his curiosity, often wasting huge amounts of time trying to find more information, more pictures, or more entertainment. Yet the Internet has nothing to do with real life—dishes to be done, people to talk to, books to be read, flowers to be picked, snowballs to be thrown, wood to be carved. The Internet disconnects our mind from work and play, people and animals—anything that is *real*. Having an unreal world to escape to for long hours is very unhealthy for all of us, especially children and teens, who are already prone to egocentrism due to their age and development. Children and teens need to focus more on serving others and on learning real, hands-on skills. They need to learn self-discipline and good work habits and be involved in active, imaginative play, rather than wasting huge chunks of time online.

Video games also create simulated realities, promoting escapism and egocentricity, encouraging an addictive, unhealthy form of competition, and fostering passive habits of mind—all serious problems for our boys especially. Moreover, the content of many games is immoral, often fostering violence, especially towards women. Video games should not form the mainstay of our sons' leisure time.

In fact, our sons would be better off without them altogether. When we decide to eliminate them from our home, we can expect a barrage of protests. However, if we stick to our decision, we will be pleased to see our boys rediscover their natural affinity for active play and creativity that is partially or completely stifled by the addiction to video games.

Similarly, children—and adults—who spend a lot of time texting or using social media spend inordinate amounts of time away from reality; many grow up without ever learning to make eye contact with the clerk at the check-out counter or to say hello to the people they pass on the street. They are exchanging simulated experiences and communications for real ones, neglecting the people actually present to them, sharing only a parody of true conversation.

Maintaining rules limiting TV, Internet, video games, and social media may be difficult, but it is vital to creating a learning environment in our home. Perhaps we could even get rid of the Internet in our home, so that the family can go online only during trips to the library. That would probably free up a surprising amount of time for activities done together: playing games, singing, reading, taking walks, or throwing a Frisbee.

The second most important factor in creating a learning environment in our home is to furnish our homes with lots of books, of all kinds: mysteries, adventures, historical fiction, novels, fantasies, biographies, science books, art books, foreign language books, poetry books, riddle books, math books, craft books, saint books, encyclopedias, solitaire books, sports books, cook books—books of every reading level, on any topic that we want our children to learn about or that our children might be interested in, from dinosaurs to knights, from the nurses to astronauts, from dolls to detectives, from flamingoes to volcanoes, from Daniel Boone to El Greco—we want to tempt our children to the enjoyable and edifying activity of reading! Comic books are about the only kind of book we may not want to encourage, but even these might be permissible if they comprise only a tiny percentage of all the books our children read.

Booksalefinder.com is a great resource for finding local used book sales. Frequent trips to the library can also be helpful. Since most libraries no longer stamp the due date on the books, we may want to keep the list of the books we've gotten out in the same place every time, and we could provide a shelf just for library books so they do not get misplaced. Marking the due date on the calendar also helps. We can visit our own library, as well as libraries in nearby towns, and order hard-to-find books through Interlibrary Loan.

Other resources for a learning environment will include fun, educational games. Nowadays there are games available in almost every level of every subject. If there is no parent/teacher store nearby, check out the astonishing selection of games at educationallearninggames.com. We can also allow our children access to basic craft supplies, map puzzles, some inexpensive science equipment, good quality music tapes or CD's, and, of course, paper, crayons, and pencils for drawing and writing. In short, any tool that helps our children develop skills, discover the world, or express their own creativity without making too big a mess, according to our own comfort level, can contribute to the learning environment in our home.

The last component of a learning environment is conversation. Conversation should be a way of life in our home. We can ask the children what they think about a book, a painting, or a movie, listening carefully to their answers, and then sharing our own opinions. Most children love compiling "favorites," so we can have discussions on our favorite color, animal, song, saint, feast day, season, book, artist, painting, poem, type of dinosaur, sports team, etc. The possibilities here are endless. The point, of course, is not to pin down each child to selecting one favorite in each category, but to generate a thoughtful discussion. We can ask each child why he has chosen his favorite, teaching him to think reflexively and to articulate. We can tell our children stories about our own childhood, our school days, our first job, how we met their father, and so forth. Most children are fascinated by the past lives of their parents. We can tell our children about current events, according to their age and maturity, about politics, and our own political leanings. We can tell them about controversies in history or religion or science—the Civil War, the Protestant Revolt, unapproved apparitions, evolution, including arguments for both sides of each issue, and explaining which side is right, and why. Many Catholic children hear a lot about Vatican II and are confused about it, especially if adults become emotional when discussing it. It's important to sit down and explain what Vatican II is and how our children should view it. If we don't know all of the facts, we can admit our ignorance and look them up in a reliable source. We can try not to brush off younger children's questions because they are difficult: What was the Inquisition? What is wrong with communism? Why don't some nuns wear habits? Why do some people go to the Latin Mass and some go to the Novus Ordo? We can help our children sift through the various facts and form their own reasonable opinions.

Teens should be given thought-provoking books. Some examples: *The Quest for Shakespeare* by Joseph Pearce; *The Screwtape Letters* or *Perelandra* by C. S. Lewis; *The Privilege of Being a Woman* by Alice von Hildebrand; *The Politically Incorrect Guide to American History* by Thomas Woods, Jr.; *How Christ Changed the World* by Luis Civardi, *The Rural Solution* by Msgr. Richard Williamson et al, or *Weapons of Mass Instruction* by John Taylor Gatto.. Moreover, parents should discuss these books with their teens. Almost any book by G. K. Chesterton will stimulate discussion; a few good choices for teens might be *The Man Who Was Thursday, Manalive*, or a few essays from *Tremendous Trifles* (which are all available from Dover Publications). If possible, we can read a book with our teen—either silently or a loud—so we can take a more intelligent part in the discussions. Does our teen find the book's arguments convincing? Why or why not? Maybe we will want to find thought-provoking articles from newspapers, magazines, or websites like catholicexchange.com or catholiclane.com, that we can cut out or print out for our teens to read and discuss with us. This way we can cover a multitude of serious—and occasionally, lighter—topics fairly painlessly. Teens will be more interested in reading contemporary articles than a heavy book and will enjoy time spent chatting with their parents.

Engaging in lively, intelligent conversation with our children, day after day, will do more than almost anything else to raise the level of their thinking—at least that is the conclusion of educators Roberta Michnick Golinkoff, Kathy Hisrch-Pasek, and Diane Ever in their book, *Einstein Never Used Flash Cards*. Conversation helps children articulate their thoughts, think through opinions to their logical conclusions, support their opinions with reasonable arguments, listen, analyze, understand another perspective, and eventually have the confidence—and competence—to form opinions on their own.

To fight burnout, it may be necessary to give children full freedom for a while and see how much they learn and accomplish on their own in a true learning environment. Some parents may prefer to keep loose reins, setting up minimum requirements, such as: read one science book a week and write a summary; play a math game and go over catechism every morning; do some form of creative writing on Mondays, correct spelling and grammar errors on Tuesdays, do a geography puzzle on Wednesdays, play a logic game on Thursdays, and do a family science experiment on Fridays. Or we can require each child to read a certain number of pages a day in any book they choose, subject to our approval. Or we may read about a different country aloud together as a family every week. Chances are, if we have made available truly interesting books and fun games, these minimum requirements won't be necessary, but having these requirements may ease our own worries about the education of our children, especially if we live in a state with stringent homeschooling requirements. We can gradually add more requirements as our children become interested in school again or as their needs change.

If we've adopted a very rigid academic program in the past, we may want to allow a few weeks of "deschooling" so our children have a chance to dissociate the idea of "learning" from "boredom"—or something worse. It may take time before our children exhibit the slightest interest in any book or game that could even remotely be considered educational. We must have patience and give them the time they need to recover from their negative feelings towards learning, without prodding or nagging them or reminding them how much money these beautiful books and games cost. Chances are, if television, Internet, video games, and other technology are not available to them, they will be learning lots, whether or not it looks like they're learning.

When we do resume lessons, if we stop using curricula, grades, and motivational methods, and substitute a learning environment, with no more than minimal requirements, such as the sample list above, then we don't need to play teacher anymore. We are just mothers again, encouraging our children, answering questions, providing basic parameters and rules—but not saddled with the full-time job of teaching our children while running a house. Homeschooling becomes much less stressful, and even fun. We get to enjoy spending time with our children, reading together, playing games, and conversing, instead of wrangling over unfinished schoolwork. Yes, we need to exert some effort to create a learning environment, but our efforts will be motivated by the pleading faces of our children, begging us to dig out a copy of the next *Little House* book or to play MathSmart just one more time. Yes, we'll be busy, but with lighter, freer hearts—overwhelmed, not by work, but by amazement at the insatiable drive to learn the Lord has given our children.

# 6

# TO GRADE OR NOT TO GRADE

*"Free curiosity has more force in our learning
things than a frightful enforcement."*

—ST. AUGUSTINE

DO we assign grades to our children's schoolwork or not? Grades are a huge part of most children's lives. But we have to ask, what impact do grades have on children?

Classroom teachers use grades because they teach so many children that they don't know which students are learning the material. Grades can also motivate children to study and learn, in order to avoid punishment for poor grades and to please parents and teachers by earning good grades.

But are grades necessary—or even desirable—in a homeschool? When we're teaching one-on-one, do we need to design a test to find out how much our child has learned? Can't we just ask him a few questions or tell the child to summarize what he's been reading? Can't we simply observe our child solving some math problems to determine if he knows what he's doing? And won't these informal conversations and observations tell us just as much as a test would—if not more—about our child's grasp of a subject without any of the detrimental effects of testing?

Testing and grading a child do have detrimental effects, the primary one being the pressure placed on the child to perform well. This pressure can cause anxiety and stress, even panic, in scrupulous or sensitive children, which, ironically, impedes their ability to focus on the material they need to learn. Stress should not play a major role in a child's life, but often it does when the emphasis of his education is placed on passing tests, instead of on teaching the child and filling his needs. Moreover, teaching our children to learn material in order to pass a test robs our homeschool of the whole concept of learning as an end in and of itself. If our children learn facts to pass a test, chances are they'll forget those facts as soon as the test is over. We've all had the experience of cramming, passing, and forgetting. Testing and grading divorces learning from real life, making learning not a natural part of living, but a business we do on the side to achieve certain grades and forget about. In short, if our children are learning material so they can do well on a test, then they won't be learning because they want to know; they won't be learning because the information is interesting or useful or worth knowing in and of itself. Tests take the joy and meaning out of learning.

Test-taking is a skill our children need to learn in order to get into college, trade school, and some professions. We may not agree with the philosophy behind standardized tests, and we may not believe in the accuracy of the results, but we still do need, at some point, to help our children be comfortable taking them. In some states, of course, children have to take standardized tests to fulfill the state's homeschooling requirements, and a few practice tests might help them feel comfortable with taking the test. However, we must be careful not to put pressure on them to score well on these tests or to lead them to associate test-taking with learning. Above all, we must not allow ourselves to tailor our homeschool curricula to performing well on standardized tests; our curricula should always be geared to our children's needs.

In high school, we may need to assign grades to compile a transcript for graduation or college admission. We may also want to administer written tests so our child can get used to them, especially if he intends to go on to a trade school or college. However, the emphasis should not be on grades. Even in high school, we can sometimes count our conversations as oral exams, as well as using term papers and projects to determine how well our child has mastered the material. Because this method can be subjective at times, we must be careful to honestly rate our child's performance instead of giving automatic A's—but because this method is so effective, we may find ourselves giving more A's than we otherwise would.

The whole matter of grading comes down to this: grades and tests may help us judge our child's performance, but grades and tests will not help our children learn. Isn't learning the goal of education? Don't we want our children to make learning an integral part of their lives, to enjoy learning, and to remember much of what they've learned? If so, tests and grades cannot form the bulwark of our homeschool.

In a sense, the intellectual life is much like the spiritual life. If we do good to avoid punishment or to earn some reward, such as to avoid hell or gain heaven, we may succeed at doing good, but it will be a tedious, joyless struggle. However, if we do good out of love for God, our struggle is transformed into a meaningful battle by the joy and satisfaction of our sacrificial love.

In both the intellectual life and the spiritual life, let us motivate ourselves and our children by love rather than fear. True, fear is a great motivator, and it has its place in short-term situations, but used over a long period of time, fear breeds resentment; in the long run, it loses its effectiveness and gives way to despair. Love, on the other hand, moves our hearts and lightens our burdens. Let us, then, motivate ourselves and our children by love, the most powerful force in the world, and transform our homeschool into a true school of love.

# 7

## TEACHING OUR CHILDREN TO THINK

*"To train a citizen is to train a critic.*
*The whole point of education is that it*
*should give a man abstract and eternal*
*standards, by which he can judge*
*material and fugitive conditions."*

—G. K. CHESTERTON

ONE of our goals as homeschoolers is to raise children who know how to think. We want to train our children to be able to form their own intelligent opinions, rather than believing anything they hear, and to be able to evaluate information and analyze its logic and coherence. We also want to raise our children to be creative and innovative; we want them to be able to come up with new ideas and solve problems by thinking beyond the conventional mold.

Teachers in public and parochial schools have found this task increasingly difficult. Why? Because many factors in modern culture, particularly our advanced entertainment technology, have dumbed us down, making us more passive in thought and in habit, and training us not to think independently. (Some might argue classroom education tends to further inculcate conformity, passivity, and non-independent thinking—though really top-notch teachers can avoid this pitfall to some extent.) One of the benefits of homeschooling, of course, is that we can operate almost independently of modern culture. We can take what is good from modern culture and eliminate the rest from our home.

The first thing we need to do to encourage critical thinking in our home is to create a learning environment, as we discussed in chapter 5. This means we need to eliminate certain forms of entertainment from our home—or at least drastically minimize their influence. We discussed the television and video games, but other things to remove can include electronic toys or games, and various forms of social media. The absence of the television and other forms of technological entertainment will force children to find more active pastimes.

Encourage reading as an alternate form of entertainment. Reading is an excellent way to develop abstract thinking. It requires the mind to translate the words on a page into mental pictures, so although it may look like a passive, sedentary occupation, and although it can be quite relaxing, it actually develops mental sharpness. Having lots of books easily accessible, making frequent trips to the library, and allowing ourselves some leisure time reading in front of the children to set a good example will promote a culture of reading in our house.

Listening develops mental powers, as well. While listening, we must translate the spoken word into mental pictures. Reading books aloud to our children, even the older ones (maybe a chapter every evening), or listening to a favorite book on tape, or purchasing some classic radio shows (check out radiospirits.com) and listening together with our children are all excellent ways to pass the time. Even listening to a sports event over the radio will develop mental powers more than watching the same event on television.

Games can also help in developing critical thinking and problem-solving skills. Strategic or logic games—such as Stratego, Connect Four, chess, Clue, Mastermind, Quoridor, or any of the many other thinking games now available—are excellent options. Games can be expensive, but it is money well spent, providing hours spent as a family, laughing, having fun, and developing critical skills. (Yard sales and thrift shops can be great places to find fun games without the expense.) Be careful to choose games that are actually fun, rather than thinly disguised classroom activities, like question-and-answer games such as Trivial Pursuit—unless some of the children actually prefer such games. Sudoku, logic puzzles, mazes, or even crosswords can be relaxing and fun, yet also good for our children's brains. (Studies have shown that older people who regularly do crossword puzzles are less likely to develop Alzheimer's disease, so they may be salutary for our youngsters' minds, as well.)

Music can also play a role in developing mental faculties. Most people know now about the studies that show that listening to classical music can provide a calming atmosphere conducive to intellectual activity. So we should play classical music in our homes. Inexpensive CDs or audio tapes of the great composers are fairly easy to find, and the local library is also a good resource. Learning to play a musical instrument has been shown to raise a child's IQ as well, probably because translating musical notation into specific notes requires great concentration and abstract thinking. Music lessons can be expensive, but unless we are aiming to raise professional concert masters, we may be able to teach our children ourselves or find a neighborhood teenager who plays a musical instrument and would be willing to give our children lessons for a fraction of the cost (or in exchange for some kind of lesson we can give them— sewing, knitting, cooking, Spanish, calculus—whatever we know how to do that the teenager wants to learn).

Conversation, as mentioned earlier, is another way to encourage critical thinking. Ask children what they think about things or why they think something happens the way it does. Discuss books, movies, songs, art, traditions, religion, philosophy, science—anything that captures our interest or theirs. Once they have thought carefully and given their opinion, affirm whatever is right in what they have said (even if the conclusion they drew was wrong), and build on that to lead them to the true answers. Of course, we must treat their ideas respectfully or they will be discouraged from sharing their ideas again; they may be even be discouraged from thinking independently again. We must silence siblings who giggle or scoff at others, and use tact to gently correct any errors. Frequent conversation with our children about their interests will do more than almost anything else to encourage analytical thought.

As our children grow older, using logic games or even a logic book can help them think clearly. *The Fallacy Detective* by homeschooling brothers Nathaniel Bluedorn and Hans Bluedorn is an entertaining but informative analysis of common logical fallacies, as well as common propaganda and advertising techniques. (The hilarious short story "Love Is a Fallacy" by Max Shulman can be a fun supplement to a logic course, and can even be read aloud.) Another helpful source for curricula that promotes analytical thinking is criticalthinking.com. The ability to reason logically is essential in today's world where so many people, their minds numbed by constant, passive TV-watching, make decisions based on emotional appeals or fallacious arguments.

Cutting off electronic entertainment venues also helps foster creative thinking. Again, if children have little or no access to the television, they will naturally turn to their own resources to make their own fun. Normally, reading will be an essential part of this fun, and writing is often a natural offshoot of reading. A child who loves to read often (though not always) tries his hand at writing. Sometimes his writing will mimic his current favorite book. This kind of imitation is part of learning; it helps us take the best of a book we love and somehow make it our own. We can provide materials for writing, drawing, and doing crafts so that our children can use their imagination and create. This doesn't require a lot of expensive materials or kits (although sometimes a well-chosen kit can be a great blessing); often, a child learns more and has more fun if he figures the project out completely by himself. However, he does need some raw materials, and we can provide these. We might be surprised at what a child can create from just some paper, cardboard, scissors, crayons, and tape or glue. The craft store can be a new favorite destination, as many simple, basic supplies are inexpensive. (Many craft stores offer discounts to teachers and homeschoolers, so remember to ask.)

Encourage creative writing. Stories, poems, letters to relatives or pen pals—there are a variety of formats that will keep children interested. Praising our children for their efforts will reap more benefits than pointing out flaws in their writing, especially at first. Games like Balderdash, Pictionary Junior, or charades can further stimulate creativity. Perhaps children can play a game where each child writes a paragraph of a story, stopping in the middle of a sentence, and the next child finishes the sentence and writes the next paragraph. (For younger children, have each child write just one sentence.) There are different versions of this game; some require each writer to read all that has been written so far before continuing, while other versions require the child to read only the last sentence. Either way, this game can be a hilarious way to have fun as a family and to develop creative thinking.

Creativity can also be stimulated by providing simple toys. Any toy that requires a battery should be viewed with suspicion. Simple toys could include, non-electronic dolls, tea sets, trucks, and blocks, which can stimulate hours of creative play. The simpler the toy, the more imagination the child will use. An empty box will ignite the imaginations of our youngsters better and longer than talking dolls or remote-controlled cars or expensive video games. Megablocks, Legos, tinker toys, or other building toys can build a child's spatial understanding, problem-solving skills, and creativity, as well as provide hours of uninterrupted fun.

All of these suggestions are simply methods to encourage our children to think analytically and creatively. Different methods work for different families, and there are many ways not mentioned here that would achieve the same goal. The point is to create an environment in our home that is conducive to thinking and creating. Games and activities that promote thought require effort, and children may resist them at first, but in the end, they will prefer these activities because they satisfy a deeper need than mindless, passive activities do. After all, we are made in the image and likeness of God because we have both an intellect and a will—and by using our intellect to think and to create we are exercising a power that is more like God's than any of our other powers, except our power to love. Furthermore, if our child is able to use his intellect to the fullest potential, he will be better armed to protect himself, and possibly others, from the poisonous modernist philosophies of relativism and materialism; he will be able to recognize and refute political propaganda; he will live a fuller, richer, and more intellectually satisfying life; and he will be better equipped to love the Lord our God with all his heart, soul, *and mind.*

# 8

## MAKING LEARNING FUN

*"The desire to know is natural to good men."*
—LEONARDO DA VINCI

THE idea of making learning fun is, in a way, rather a ridiculous concept because, like thinking and creating, learning is one of the most exciting and naturally satisfying activities known to man. Children learn from the time they are born without any outside motivation; they learn to breastfeed, roll over, sit up, walk, and talk without being given stickers or other tools to motivate them. Once they learn to talk, they discover that they can learn even more by asking, "Why?" to their own delight and their parents' exasperation. However, in our society, children eventually come to think of learning as a boring, tedious task involving dull textbooks and unending piles of worksheets. All too often, school teaches them that learning is dull because the children know they're in school to learn, and they find school dull. Thus, they equate learning with boredom. Giving children rewards like stickers or candy for reading or writing further convinces them that reading and writing are unenjoyable; otherwise, why would they need to be rewarded for doing these things? We, as homeschooling parents, hoping to encourage our children to learn, and perhaps remembering our own toilsome schooldays, seek to make learning fun, but a better way to approach learning might be just to avoid making learning "unfun."

This does not mean that every academic subject will be equally agreeable to all our children or that rewards are never appropriate. Some lessons are hard to learn, and a sticker or a holy card can encourage a struggling child. But let us not imitate the many educators, who, desperate to get our television-crazy children to read, come up with elaborate reward systems to persuade their students to read. In a homeschool, rewarding a child for reading is generally counterproductive. Reading is one of the great joys in life; from the time a child begins to read the simplest "I Can Read" books, reading is a privilege and a pleasure. We don't reward a child for eating cake or for playing a game—why should we reward a child for reading a book?

If a child is really struggling with reading and does not find reading a new word motivation enough, then we might want to consider whether we are pushing him to read too young. Not all children are ready to read at the age of five or six, especially boys. Forcing them when they are not interested or not ready may only cause them to hate reading, probably for years, and possibly for the rest of their lives. Waiting a year or two, until the child expresses an interest on his own, could save hours of anguish for both parent and child. Experience has shown that children who learn to read at an older age catch up with their peers very quickly. Soon they are reading at the same level as other schoolchildren their age, and they have not been taught to hate reading by being forced to learn prematurely.

To make learning fun, we need to move away from the whole concept that learning is normally not fun. The truth is fascinating, amazing, surprising, absorbing, and enthralling—if presented well. Many families find that textbooks do not tend to present the truth in an engaging manner and use instead what Charlotte Mason called "living books"— books written by one or two people, rather than by a committee, in which the author is able to build a relationship with the reader and share his passionate interest in the subject. There is a plethora of living books available for children in subjects usually considered dull. For example, *Tiger Math* by Ann Whitehead Nagda and Cindy Bickel shows children how to use various graphs to track the growth of a tiger cub in a zoo. *How Much Can a Bare Bear Bear?* by Brian Cleary amuses the reader while teaching him about homonyms and homophones. D'Aulaire's *George Washington*, Robert Lawson's *Mr. Revere and I*, Virginia Frances Voigt's *Patriots' Gold* or Alice Turner Curtis' *Little Maid of Philadelphia* might interest a child more than a chapter in a textbook on the American Revolution. Living books can be fiction or non-fiction; either way, a living book is charmingly written, engages interest, and broadens minds. The truth is not boring; it only becomes boring when presented in a tedious format. Homonyms are fun, although you'd never guess it while reading a grammar book. History is fascinating, but often history textbooks are not. It requires effort to find living books on the subjects we want our children to learn, but we won't have to test our children to see if they've read it. We'll know they have, because they'll be bubbling over with their amazement, laughter, and excitement.

Eliminating textbooks can be scary sometimes, and we may wonder, will we cover everything? We don't need to worry. Even school teachers don't always cover everything in the classroom—do you remember how often our teachers didn't finish a textbook in any given subject in one school year? Besides, having the material presented to a child doesn't necessarily mean that the child is learning it, and children tend to forget a good deal of what they're taught anyway once the test is over. However, by homeschooling with hands-on lessons and living books, our children will be much more likely to really grasp and remember the information that they do learn. Sometimes, of course, the children will not be learning exactly what their peers in public school are learning at their age; in fact, some children tend to focus on only one subject for an extended period of time, rather than doing a little bit of every subject every day. If our goal is for our children to learn and truly understand the material in their own way, rather than seeking the approval of the school board or relatives, then we will accommodate ourselves to the style of learning that works best for them, and put aside our fears of academic inferiority.

If our state requires samples of the children's work, we may occasionally need to supplement our relaxed method of instruction with a few worksheets. Alternately, we could require our child to write summaries of what he has learned on a particular topic or make up a timeline for the period he is studying in history. We may also need to use worksheets occasionally to prepare our children for state-mandated standardized tests. However, worksheets can be the exception, used primarily to fulfill state requirements, not the usual method of our homeschool. After all, if we really believe that a more relaxed method of homeschooling will help our children to learn better, then we have no reason to fear; the standardized tests will demonstrate that the children are indeed learning what they need to know. If, of course, a child does not score well on a standardized test, we can always let him take it again, after some further preparation. But we should remember that any score above 50 percent is above the national average, and therefore testifies to our success as homeschoolers.

Actually, in a study released in 2009 by the National Home Education Research Institute, homeschoolers of all educational styles scored an average of 86 percent on standardized tests. The researchers studied homeschoolers of all styles, from those who follow curricula strictly to radical unschoolers who allow their children to initiate all their academic experiences, and everything in between. Surprisingly to many people, the researchers found that the educational methods had no significant effect on the children's scores. Here is proof that relaxed homeschooling and unschooling work just as well as conventional homeschooling! Families who would like a more relaxed approach to homeschooling but are hesitant to relinquish all textbooks might be interested in Catholic Heritage Curricula (chcweb.com), which offers Catholic curricula that are less rigid, more flexible, more fun, and easier to use than many standard curriculum providers—while also reinforcing the Catholic faith in every lesson.

Of course, worksheets may be useful at times in any subject. And if we happen to come across a textbook that is well written and fun to read, we should grab it! We can keep in mind, too, that some children really enjoy worksheets and textbooks. But if worksheets and textbooks are the exception, not the rule, in our homeschool, then we won't have to worry about making learning fun—learning will be a natural activity in our house, going on all day long, often without our knowing it. While at times it may be confusing or difficult or messy, it will always be plenty of fun!

# 9

# TEACHING THE BASICS

*"Any subject can be made interesting, and*
*therefore any subject can be made boring."*

—HILAIRE BELLOC

MANY homeschooling families today are attracted to Charlotte Mason's concept of living books. However, actually getting rid of textbooks and using living books in every subject can be a little frightening, especially if we do not know anyone else who homeschools this way. Here are a few suggestions for getting started in the basic subjects.

We'll begin with math, possibly the most intimidating subject to tackle without a textbook. In fact, many families eschew textbooks in every other subject, but go back to conventional schooling methods for math. Because math requires so much memorization, as well as constant practice if we don't want to forget what we've learned, textbooks and workbooks may seem like the most practical tools to teach math. However, even with math, there are other options. Math wrap-ups are a fun, hands-on, self-correcting tool to drill math facts. Moreover, nowadays there are numerous math games available in stores. Check out educationallearninggames.com to find games that teach just about any skill in math (or any other subject). Also keep an eye out for math games at yard sales and thrift shops. "MathSmart" is a relatively inexpensive but fun way to practice math facts, with cards dealing with addition, subtraction, multiplication, division, or fractions. Educational Insights puts out self-correcting math puzzles, which can be used over and over again to practice math facts. The selection is almost endless. Of course, games are expensive, and we can't buy a game for every concept we want to teach. If we're short of funds, we can use a little imagination and make up our own games, or look for a book that gives ideas for games we can make at home, such as *Family Math* by Jean Kerr Stenmark, Virginia Thompson, and Ruth Cossey. Any game that requires the players to keep score—even Rummy 500—can provide an opportunity for arithmetic. Cribbage helps reinforce addition skills, as does the solitaire game Pyramid. Another option might be playing War, but instead of the person with the high card winning the other person's card, we could say whoever adds the two numbers (or multiplies the two numbers) and says the answer first, wins the other's card. This works best if we have two children close in age so the same child won't win every time. We may want to remove the face cards for this version of War, or we can make up our own deck of cards without face cards.

Any time we see a chart or a graph—whether it be a pie graph from an appeal from a charitable organization, which shows how donations are spent, to our heating bills which show how much gas or electricity we used each month—we can show it to our children and help them interpret it. Then we can ask them to make a similar chart or graph about something in their lives—for example, make a graph of the ages of everyone in the house, or a pie chart showing how many family members have blue, brown, or hazel eyes. Children are often interested in their parents' mail and will feel privileged at this glimpse of adult life. Also, anytime a real math problem comes up in real life, we can sit down with our children and figure it out together. When they see a real use for a skill, like how to add or subtract, our children will be more eager to master it.

We can look for living books in the subject of mathematics, too, from picture books to chapter books, including *Tiger Math*, mentioned above; *Math-terpieces* by Greg Tang; *Anno's Math Games* by Mitsumas Anno; *The Man Who Counted* by Malba Tahan; *Venn Diagrams* by Robert Froman and other books in the Young Math Book series; *What's Your Angle, Pythagoras?* by Julie Ellis; the *Sir Cumference* books by Cindy Neuschwander; *Math for Kids and Other People, Too!* or *Penrose the Mathematical Cat*, both by Theoni Pappas. *Carry On, Mr. Bowditch!* by Jean Lee Latham is the fascinating, true story of one man's practical usage of arithmetic (although the book itself contains no math). And there are many more, which we can look for at the library.

Children can learn a lot about fractions from cooking and baking. We could also make cards that have equivalent fractions, decimals, percentages, and diagrams (which show, for example, one half of a pie, one fourth of a pie, etc.), and play "Go Fish" with them.

A good game to teach borrowing and carrying involves making our own board: first, draw a winding path made up of red, blue, and yellow squares. Mark some of the red squares with plus signs and others with minus signs. Then, give each person a piece of paper and a pencil and start with 50 points each. At his turn, each player will roll a die and move his man the appropriate number of squares. If he lands on a blue square, he adds the number shown on the die; if he lands on a yellow square, he subtracts the number shown on the die; if he lands on a red square, he doubles the number and either adds or subtracts it, depending on the symbol on that square. When the first person reaches the end of the board, whoever has the highest score wins. To prevent discouragement, we can say that anyone who reaches zero or below during the game automatically wins. Children learn to borrow and carry without even realizing it using this game.

With a little imagination, we can make up games to reinforce multiplication, division, and word problems, as well. For example, we could make a board covered with squares of repeating colors, perhaps the colors of the rainbow. Each square should also have written on it the answer to a division or multiplication fact (or, for more advanced players, the answers to long division or multiplication word problems). Some squares may have the same number, as long as they are not the same color. Then we make up a stack of cards with the multiplication, division, or word problems we want our children to master. (For word problems, we can be creative, using characters from our children's favorite books, or using their favorite saints, or even using our children's names.) Lastly, cut out a bunch of small pieces of colored paper, the same colors as the squares on the board. Now we are ready to begin. Each player takes a turn, picking up a card with a math problem on it. He figures out the answer and places his man on a square on the board with the correct answer, and he collects a piece of paper that is the color of that square. The first player to win one paper of each color wins. (Trading pieces of paper in between turns is allowed.) It sounds complicated, but it really works, as children love collecting the different colored pieces of paper.

We can also keep on hand a plastic clock to help the little ones learn to tell time; Cuisenaire rods or an abacus for hands-on arithmetic; and games that develop our children's spatial understanding, such as tangrams, chess, or Othello. For learning money values, we can buy games like Moneywise Kids, Careers, and Monopoly, which help children make change for paper money, and Loose Change, which helps children add up coins. Of course, we can always design our own play money and make up our own buying and selling games. We could even keep a box of real change for the children to play store with; the opportunity to play with real money will enthrall younger children and pave the way to teaching them how to make change. We can suggest that our children make play money and hold

auctions to sell things that they were going to throw out to
their brothers and sisters. This can also be a little lesson in
economics, as for example, when they see that the value of
their play money drops when they make too much.

Some children will enjoy math more when they can
sing their math facts. Bywayofthefamily.com sells tapes and
CD's called "You Never Forget What You Sing," which
help children learn addition, subtraction, multiplication,
and division facts with music. There are so many ways to
help children learn math!

Science scares off many homeschooling mothers, too.
However, science is fascinating to children; we just need
to encourage their natural curiosity. Filling our house with
books about animals, outer space, the human body, magnets, water, plants, volcanoes, insects, dinosaurs, and other
scientific topics will be a great start. (However, we should
check animal books for inappropriate information on animals' mating habits, and books on the human body for
too much information about the reproductive system—
we might be surprised at how revealing some "children's"
books can be! Also, watch out for books that propagate
misleading information about evolution. If the book is
truly worthwhile except for one or two pages, we could
cut out the pages or use black magic marker or white-out
to obliterate objectionable sections, or we could glue the
objectionable pages together. We should try to find at least
one or two books with a Christian perspective of evolution and discuss them with each child.) We can try to find
inexpensive materials, such as a secondhand microscope

or telescope, a magnifying glass, magnets, or a flashlight, for the children to fool around with. Books with simple experiments for children abound, but if we have real science-phobia, we can purchase a few science kits to smooth the way.

We may want to tell our children to pick a science experiment from a book (subject to our approval) and have them do it alone, coming to us only if they need help. This relieves us of the burden of coordinating experiments and lessons, and micromanaging every detail. Moreover, children will enjoy the experiment more—and learn more—if they feel that they're in charge. Children can be allowed to play around with materials, too—with reasonable safety rules, of course. Furthermore, keeping a vegetable garden or growing a potted plant inside the house, hanging up a birdfeeder and identifying or sketching the birds that come, or even caring for a pet are all activities that qualify as hands-on science class. Occasionally we can have the children write a short report on the experiments, stating what they did, what resulted, and what they learned from those results, especially if we have to give the school district a sampling of the children's work. We can also have our children copy diagrams of the inside of a plant or the digestive system or the solar system, etc., from their science books. Many children will enjoy drawing the diagrams, and most will learn the lesson better for having to recreate it on paper for themselves.

Second and third graders will enjoy naturalist Thornton Burgess's delightful books, in which animals talk like people while acting according to the habits of their species. *The Adventures of Reddy Fox* or *The Adventures of Little Joe Otter* are good ones to start with. (Dover Publications has reprinted Burgess's books with fewer of the original illustrations but at an exceptionally low price.) The *Step-Up* Books are also excellent, easy readers for second and third graders, with titles like *Animals Do the Strangest Things, Insects Do the Strangest Things,* etc. Other excellent science books to keep an eye out for include *Your Body and How It Works* by Patricia Lauber; *The Sick Book* by Marie Winn; *Seaside and Wayside* by Julia McNair Wright; *Archimedes and the Door of Science* by Jeanne Bendick; *Find the Constellations* by H. A. Rey; and *Mystery of the Periodic Table* by Benjamin D. Wiker. The out-of-print Junior Science Books provide clear, intriguing explanations on a wide variety of topics, including electricity, trees, light, magnets, sound, icebergs, and stars. Keep a look-out at used book sales for books by Herbert S. Zim. His books for younger readers cover scientific facts about different animals, while his upper grade level books examine different parts of the body, such as *Your Brain and How It Works, Blood, Bones,* and *Your Stomach and Digestive System.* A more recent author and illustrator, Jim Arnosky, has produced books on wildlife for several different age levels, from pre-schoolers to upper grade school, which are both informative and gorgeously illustrated.

For the most part, don't worry too much about whether a science book is too easy; as long as our child is learning new information, he is benefiting. Moreover, if there is a lot of new information or new concepts in the book, a child may understand better if the reading level is easier than the level he is reading for literature. If our child continually chooses science books on the same topic, we may want to require him to choose a book on some other scientific topic so that he learns some science besides dinosaurs, for example, but still retains some say in his book selection.

Unfortunately, evolution is a dominant topic in many children's science books. We should make sure our children understand that evolution is a theory, although writers usually present it as proven fact, and that there is much evidence against it. Because most books arguing against evolution are written for adults, we may have difficulty finding books for children that present science from a non-evolutionary perspective. There are some non-Catholic resources available, but we must be careful that they contain no anti-Catholic bias. (One Protestant book on anatomy states that its goal is to explain anatomy from a "Great Reformation" perspective!) However, if we look, we may be able to find some Christian, non-Catholic, books that teach science from a non-evolutionary perspective with minimal religious discussion, such as *The Great Dinosaur Mystery and the Bible* by Paul S. Taylor for grade school children, and *The Geology Book* by Dr. John D. Morris for junior high, and *Creation Facts of Life* by Gary Parker for high schoolers. We can just glance over the religious portion in these books and discuss it with our children. Hopefully, someday, a Catholic will write science books for children that show evolution in its proper perspective so we don't have to choose between Protestant theology and atheistic empiricism in our science books.

Furthermore, we must emphasize to our children that science books or magazines which portray man as evil for destroying the earth are also imparting a biased perspective. While it is true that man should be a good steward of the marvelous earth God has created, we must also remember that God did create the earth for man's use, and man's real needs should preempt concerns about nature.

History is another subject we want our children to learn, and there are many wonderful books we can have on hand for them. Some mothers may also be nervous about remembering all the important events and dates in history, but history is easy to make fun—after all, history is essentially a story, and children love stories. As discussed earlier, historical fiction and biographies can supplement or replace textbooks. The Discovery Books and the Childhood of Famous Americans are two series of biographies for second, third, and fourth graders that really make historical figures come alive. Many libraries have a good selection of both series. A few helpful biographies for European history for upper grade school children include *Son of Charlemagne* by Barbara Willard; *Quest for a King: Searching for the Real King Arthur* by Catherine M. Andronik; *Leonardo da Vinci* by Emily Hahn; and *Napoleon and the Battle of Waterloo* by Frances Winwar. The last two books mentioned are from the superb Landmark Book series, some of which are still in print, while out-of-print copies of the others are fairly easy to locate at libraries, used book sales, and used book stores. This series can be used for upper grade school through high school.

Other helpful resources include the "Cornerstones of Freedom" series, most of which are written by R. Conrad Stein, which tell about specific events in American history; Jean Fritz's playful but informative books, like *And Then What Happened, Paul Revere?*; and Ingri and Edgar Parin D'Aulaire's beautifully illustrated biographies of Leif Ericson, Ben Franklin, George Washington, Buffalo Bill, and Abraham Lincoln. Emmanuel Books offers *If You Sailed on the Mayflower in 1620* and other books in the "If You . . ." series that use a delightful question-and-answer format to teach the reader about how people lived in different time periods.

The Catholic Treasury Books are out of print, but worth the extra effort of searching for them, as they provide exciting, easy-to-read, true stories from both American and European history with a Catholic perspective. Bethlehem Books, a division of Ignatius Press that reprints quality historical fiction for Catholic homeschoolers, has actually reprinted one Catholic Treasury Book, *Red Hugh, Prince of Donegal*. Other titles, still out of print, that are worth looking for at abe.com or amazon.com would include: *Simon O' the Stock*, *The Marylanders*, and *Charity Goes to War*, all by Anne Heagney; *Alfred of Wessex* by Frank Morris; *The Quiet Flame* by Eva Betz; *A Candle for Our Lady* and *Bright Banners*, both by Regina Victoria Hunt; *Medicine for Wildcat* by Robert Riordan; *Desert Padre* by John Thayer; and *A Hand Raised at Gettysburg* by Grace and Harold Johsnon. Some of the "We Were There" books are still in print, such as *We Were There with Lewis and Clark* by James Munves, while many libraries and used book sales carry the out-of-print titles. This engaging series for middle grade school children portrays fictional children observing true historical events. For high school, two excellent, well-written texts are Anne Carroll's *Christ the King, Lord of History* and *Christ and the Americas*.

There are also numerous books on ancient civilization, such as: *The Gift of the River: A History of Ancient Egypt* by Enid LaMonte Meadowcroft; *The Pharaohs of Ancient Egypt* by Elizabeth Payne; *The Golden Days of Greece* by Olivia Coolidge; *D'Aulaire's Book of Greek Myths* by Ingri and Edgar Parin D'Aulaire; *The Romans* by Alfred Duggan; *Swords, Spears and Sandals* by Richard Suskind; *Julius Caesar* by John Gunther. All of these are non-fiction, living books which could form the bulwark of our curriculum on ancient history. *Mara, Daughter of the Nile* by Eloise Jarvis MacGraw or *Detectives in Togas* by Henry Winterfeld are wonderful novels that will reinforce our ancient civilization lessons. Rosemary Sutcliff has written children's versions of *The Iliad* and *The Odyssey*, entitled *Black Ships before Troy* and *The Wanderings of Odysseus*, which may enhance our study of ancient Greece. Picture books can be educational, too; after reading *The Great Alexander the Great* by Joe Lasker or *Hannibal and his 37 Elephants* by Marilyn Hirsh, no child will forget either historical figure (although we may decide to censor some of the arguments in Hannibal's belligerent family). *The Puzzle of Ancient Man* by Donald

E. Chittick or *Secrets of the Lost Races* by Rene Noorbergen
will give our high schoolers a new and intriguing perspective on ancient civilizations.

If we want, we can occasionally tell our children to
write a summary of what they learned from their reading. Children who really resist writing could be required
to write a list of "things I learned from this book," which
may be less intimidating than composing a summary.
Other options could include having the children give an
oral report in front of the family about a topic, or write a
short story about people who witnessed a certain historic
event, or compose some diary entries supposedly written by
a person living in the time period we are studying. These
activities may be more interesting to a child than answering
"Comprehension Questions" at the end of every chapter in
a textbook, but they still provide proof to our school district
that we are teaching history, as well as allowing our children the chance to assimilate the material and make it their
own. Hanging a time-line on the wall that includes periods
covered by many books will reinforce the dates even more
because our children see them continually. An artistic child
may want to make a small poster of each of the historical
figures he is studying, with drawings, accompanied by dates
of the most important events of the person's life. We could
also make up a crossword puzzle about a historical event or
person, or find one on-line that is free to print and use. If we
don't feel up to making a crossword puzzle, we could have
our children make up their own (and photocopy it for their
younger siblings to do when they study the same material).

Historical fiction, as well as non-fiction, personal stories, can impress historical facts into our heads with even greater effectiveness. For example, if we are covering World War II with grade school children, we can look for *Twenty and Ten* by Claire Huchet Bishop, *Snow Treasure* by Marie McSwigan, or *The Winged Watchman* by Hilda Van Stockum—three hard-to-put-down books about children during the war. Teens will be captivated by *Paris Underground* by Etta Shiber or *The Raft* by Robert Trumbull, which are both fascinating, first-hand accounts of World War II. Biographies of saints who lived during that time, such as *St. Maxmilian Kolbe* by Fr. J. J. Smith, published by TAN Books, or *St. Edith Stein: Blessed by the Cross*, published by Pauline Books and Media, will blend history and faith, and help our children understand the relation between religion and politics.

If we own a television, we can find movies that portray different historical time periods. One great example is *The Scarlet and the Black*, an excellent movie for older children about Monsignor O'Flaherty, who helped rescue Jews and other refugees during World War II. Unfortunately, the movie briefly depicts Pope Pius XII as weak in his dealings with the Nazis, which is definitely not true, so we would have to emphasize to our children the truth about Pope Pius XII. Other movies about World War II would include *The Man Who Never Was* with Clifton Webb (as well as the book by the same name); *Thirty Seconds Over Tokyo* with Spencer Tracy (again, first check out the book by the same name); *Destination Tokyo*, with Cary Grant, or, for more light-hearted fare, *Buck Privates*. If we look, we can find similar resources for all the different historical time periods that we want our children to learn about.

Another helpful website is doverpublications.com, which sells coloring books and paper dolls of many historical figures and events. We can also look into historical festivals or Civil War reenactments or historical museums to make history come alive for our youngsters, or we can do related crafts. Emmanuel Books sells kits providing the materials and instructions to make cornhusk dolls, coon tail caps, tomahawks, quill feather pens, fringe pouches, and more. Libraries often offer books featuring crafts related to different time periods, such as *Ancient Egypt: A Civilization Project Book* by Susan Purdy. Alternately, Gillian Chapman has written a series called "Crafts from the Past," on the ancient civilizations of Egypt, China, Rome, Greece, the Aztecs, and the Indians. Similarly, David C. King has done a series of books with projects, games, activities, and recipes on colonial days, pioneer days, revolutionary days, Civil War days, Wild West days, World War II days, Victorian days, and probably more. Nomad Press has also published several historical craft books, such as *Medieval Projects You Can Do!* by Marsha Groves and *Great Colonial America Projects You Can Build Yourself!* by Kris Bordessa, and other titles on Civil War projects, World War II projects, and Leonardo da Vinci inventions. Likewise, Rosemary Chorzempa's *Design Your Own Coat of Arms: an Introduction to Heraldry* might help our medieval history lesson come alive. While choosing history books, especially medieval history, we must be wary of anti-Christian bias. With this in mind, we should be able to find hands-on books for whatever period of history we are covering, and we could leave it out to subtly entice our child. Another idea is to tell our child to choose one craft and complete it as a part of lessons. Finding these books in the library or through inter-library loan would be a less expensive way to use them, since we may be needing several during the course of a single year.

There are many ways to teach geography, too. There is a plethora of geography games that are both educational and fun, including *Snapshots Across America, Name That Country, Great States, Scrambled States,* and *Landmark Bingo*. We could even make our own geography game, and our children might learn even more if they help design it. For example, we could glue pictures and small maps of different countries onto index cards, with little facts about the country written underneath each picture. When we have at least three or four cards per country, we could then play "World Rummey," with each player trying to get three or more cards about the same country. Old encyclopedias are a great source for the pictures, or we could print them off the Internet, or our budding artist could draw them. Map puzzles are a fabulous, hands-on way to teach the location of different states or countries; these can be found at maps. com or abroaderview.com.

Reading books that take place in other countries can help familiarize children with the world around them, as well as reading biographies of famous people and saints who lived in different countries. For example, *Little Pear* by Eleanor Frances Lattimore is an early chapter book about a little Chinese boy, while *Young Fu of the Upper Yangtze* by Elizabeth Foreman Lewis would entertain and educate older readers about China. Several books by Alta Halverson Seymour, such as *Erik's Christmas Camera*, are about children in different European countries. *St. Rose of Lima* by Mary Fabyan Windeatt tells us about the saintly girl who lived in Peru; *Afiong* by Mother Eleanor deals with the first Holy Communion of a girl in Africa; and *Edel Quinn: Beneath the Southern Cross* by Evelyn M. Brown tells of an Irish missionary to Africa. Many libraries carry Virginia Haviland's "Favorite Fairy Tales Told in . . ." books, which tell legends and fairy tales popular in different cultures, while *The Case of the Marble Monster and Other Tales* by I. G. Edmonds will give youngsters a marvelous taste of Japanese wisdom and humor. Primary grade children might enjoy *Let There Be Llamas!* by Virginia Kroll, which introduces the reader to children from all over the world. *Our Friends from Other Lands* by the Daughters of St. Paul is a gem of a textbook that is particularly hard to find but worth the effort, as children love rereading the stories of saints and other Catholic boys and girls from different countries.

Even picture books can be fun and educational for both young and old. For example, *Guard Mouse* by Don Freeman is a picture book that takes the reader on an exciting tour of London; *The Boy at the Dike* by Marguerite Scott teaches the child the importance of dikes in Holland;

*Ferdinand* by Munro Leaf reveals the drama of a Spanish bull ring; and *The Empty Pot* by Demi gives the reader a taste of Oriental thought. These and other picture books will bring geography to life for our grade school students and our preschoolers will enjoy listening in, too. Some of these listed here are in print, and some are not, but a little research will help us find these and other books about various countries all over the world. Many libraries offer the "Count Your Way Through . . ." series by James Haskins, which teaches children not just about the numbers in different countries, but a little about their culture, too. Many libraries also have the "Fiesta" series about the various feast days celebrated in different countries.

In addition to finding good books on different countries, we can hang up maps in our kitchen or dining room or keep a globe easily accessible; then, whenever we see or hear the name of a place in the course of the day—while reading a saint's life, or a history book, or while looking at the labels of the fruit we're eating—we can locate the place on our maps. Perhaps we can have a race to see who can find the place first. If we are studying a specific state or country, we can have our children draw a map of the state or country, marking off the capital city, the largest river, and other important cities or mountain ranges. Catholic Heritage Curricula offers a non-consumable program called "1001 Facts for Your Catholic Geography Bee" on the United States, which can be adapted for children in different grade levels. They also offer "Uncle Josh's Outline Maps," which includes reproducible line maps for children to use when designing their own maps. Dover Publications offers coloring books with mazes of different states and countries, which provide a fun reinforcement to what our children have learned.

For world history, we could design a form for our children to fill out about each country, with places to write down the country's capital city, language, religion, natural landmarks, man-made landmarks, exports, foods, customs, and a place to draw the country's flag. Then we could get a book out of the library on a different country every week, and have the children use the book to fill in the form. That would be a very interactive but low-stress way to introduce our child to world geography, and occasionally we can try a recipe or craft from the country our child is studying.

We've listed a lot of resources to bring academic subjects alive in our homes—but we don't need to worry about buying them all! Children can only use so many materials and absorb so much information at once, and we can only afford so much at once. Gradually, we can build up supplies and books for all the subjects, over a period of years, all the while keeping an eye out at yard sales or at parent-teacher stores for worthwhile bargains and taking advantage of the local library and inter-library loan system.

Eventually, by using different learning tools, we will relax and realize that homeschooling and learning really can be a fun, enjoyable way to spend time together. Teaching and learning are natural activities that parents and children have been sharing for centuries—and that we have been sharing with our children since their birth. We don't need a degree in education or an expensive curriculum or anything except a little bit of patience and a lot of love. Once we begin to enjoy homeschooling, we can be sure that our children will enjoy it, too.

# 10

## CONFIDENCE

*"God does not command impossibilities,*
*but by commanding admonishes you to do*
*what you can and to pray for what you cannot,*
*and aids you that you may be able."*

—ST. AUGUSTINE

AS homeschoolers, so often we encounter mothers who say they would love to homeschool—but they can't. Their reasons vary from a lack of education to a lack of organizational skills, but usually what it all comes down to is a lack of confidence. Even within homeschooling circles, many mothers struggle with self-doubt. Are we capable of educating our children? Are we doing a good job? Do we have enough wisdom, patience, and intelligence to cover all the information our children need to learn? Have we chosen the best teaching style for our family? Some mothers would like to homeschool with a more relaxed, hands-on approach, but they are afraid to let go of a rigid curriculum. They fear that if they forego seemingly omniscient textbooks, they won't "cover everything." They worry that relatives, friends, or the school district will find their children's education inadequate. They lack the confidence to direct their children's education themselves.

Let's examine both of these situations separately. First, can the average mother homeschool successfully? Or must the homeschooling mother possess superior education, organizational skills, time management, heroic patience, and so forth? Must she be able to recite everything she learned in every class in high school? First of all, studies show that homeschooling children outperform students in conventional schools regardless of their parents' level of education. We don't need to remember everything we learned during high school to teach our children. Furthermore, while organizational skills and patience are helpful to a homeschooling mother, any mother can develop these qualities if she tries, and homeschooling is a great way to start. If a mother with a child in a conventional school worries that she can't manage housework and homeschooling combined, she can consider that if she spends an hour or two helping her child with homework, then she already spends about the same amount of time teaching her child that most homeschoolers do; after all, teaching one-on-one is a very efficient method and requires dramatically less time. Besides, she can help her child in the morning, when both are fresh, instead of in the evening when the whole family is tired after a long day. If the mother is not spending much time helping her child with homework, then her child is probably good at working independently and may not require as much one-on-one attention. Most children who can read can do most of their lessons on their own if a schedule is written out for them; we can certainly find time to check their work, answer a question, or find a new bottle of glue upon request, and this is much less intimidating or time-consuming than sitting and teaching each subject to each child.

Yes, housework may suffer when we homeschool. Of course, our house needn't look like a pig pen; after all, children can help out with the housework—something they'd never have time for if they were at school all day and doing homework all evening. Nevertheless, the house necessarily will be messier when our children spend the whole day at home. So we need to ask ourselves, is our children's education worth the sacrifice? Surely our children's intellectual, emotional, and spiritual well-being is worth a little clutter and dust.

If we are concerned about not covering all the academic material at home, perhaps we should be more worried about what else our children would be learning at school— the crass language, impure jokes, materialistic attitudes, social cliques, bullying, and politically correct ideology. Simply by keeping our children at home, we are protecting them from all kinds of bad influences and unhealthy peer pressure. What our children won't learn by not going to school will benefit our children's spiritual and emotional formation exponentially. Besides, despite our feelings of ineptitude, there's no reason to believe our child's academic experience will have to be sacrificed one iota. On the contrary, at home children are not distracted by classmates' gossip or lack of discipline; they are not embarrassed to ask questions if they don't understand; and they can cover material slowly or quickly, depending on their own grasp of the subject. Homeschoolers benefit enormously from having one-on-one attention from an adult whenever they need it, and they are free to adapt the lessons to their own interests and learning styles. For all of these reasons and more, homeschooling students continually surpass their peers in virtually every academic level, regardless of their parents' level of education, as was most recently confirmed by the study conducted by the National Home Education Research Institute in 2009.

We need to put to rest our fears about "covering everything." No teacher or school system covers everything the child should know, and our country's current school system is worse than most, often graduating high school seniors who can barely read and write. If we manage to pass on the basics to our children, as well as a deep love of learning and the tools they need to find out whatever we've omitted, then we have successfully homeschooled our children. If, in addition, we've brought up our children in a loving, affirming atmosphere and taught them to live their faith in their everyday lives, then we've achieved our ultimate goal as Catholic parents. "Covering everything" is impossible and irrelevant. If our children have a desire to learn, the ability to research, and sufficient confidence in themselves, they can figure out whatever they need to know to succeed in life.

Some mothers may fear that homeschooling costs too much for their budget. Admittedly, if we are staying home with our children, we can't be out earning money at the same time. However, although we're not bringing in a salary, homeschooling doesn't need to cost a lot of money. We don't need to purchase expensive, new textbooks in every subject every year to homeschool. Furthermore, while store-bought science kits and educational games can enhance a homeschool, they are certainly not necessary. Children's books are easy to find secondhand, and if we look, we can sometimes find educational games or science equipment that way, too. We can also make up our own educational games. An old set of encyclopedias—which can be purchased inexpensively at used book sales—can provide a huge array of pictures that we can cut up for a board game or for cards for our own history, geography or science games. (Old encyclopedia pictures can also be used for decorating reports, timelines, notebooks, folders, or stationery.) We will discuss more ways to homeschool on a budget later on; for now, we will just comment that homeschooling does not need to be an expensive endeavor, as long as we are willing to put in a little time and use some ingenuity.

What about the fears of homeschoolers who lack the confidence to adopt a more relaxed educational style? We need to decide what we want the driving force behind our homeschool to be—a love of learning, or a fear of authority. In some ways, departing from conventional curricula can be more work; we need to find interesting books on every subject we want our children to learn, every era in history, every mathematical concept, etc., and there's always the possibility that we'll miss something. Yet in other ways it's easier because we don't have to waste time motivating or rewarding our children for learning, and grading worksheets and tests. Best of all, the contest of wills between the determined mother and the obstinate child is greatly diminished, and often completely eliminated. Even if we do miss a few things, we can feel sure that what our children have learned they will retain longer because the information has become alive for them. What good does it do to expose our children to a perfectly complete curriculum if they absorb only a fraction of it due to peer pressure, apathy towards school, and lack of classroom discipline? Isn't it better to expose them to most of the information they need to learn and actually make sure they learn it in a comfortable, one-on-one learning environment, while at the same time equipping them with the skills and confidence to learn whatever "essential" facts we have left out when they realize they need to know them?

Do we doubt our ability to find "living books" for our children? If we are not well-read ourselves, there are many resources available to help us find appropriate books— resources such as *Reading the Saints* by Janet McKenzie (a guide to specifically Catholic books, primarily on the saints, both in-print and out-of-print, with a chart showing historical eras and grade levels of recommended books); *For the Love of Literature* by Maureen Wittman (specifically designed for Catholic homeschooling families, this book features lists of living books that are still in print, covering all subjects in the curricula); or *A Picture Perfect*

*Childhood* by Cay Gibson (written by a Catholic for people of all faiths, this book lists picture books that can brighten our daily lessons, on the principle that picture books are not just for pre-schoolers but can inform and delight older children, as well). For homeschooling mothers not confident in their knowledge of children's literature, these three books will be a mine of information.

A look through some trustworthy Catholic homeschooling catalogs such as TAN Books/St. Benedict Press, Emmanuel Books, Bethlehem Books, Hillside Education, Ecce Homo Press, Sophia Institute Press, By Way of the Family, Mother of Our Savior, or Catholic Heritage Curricula can also help. All of these resources can assist us in finding reliable Catholic books that will engage our children's interest while teaching them at the same time. HomeschoolingBooks.com and visionforum.com are Christian, though not Catholic, resources for homeschoolers that may be helpful in supplying science or math products (though we must be careful of Protestant bias in literature, history, and religion.) Dover Publications offers a plethora of inexpensive children's literature, children's science books, children's piano books of classical music, Irish music, cowboy songs, and ragtime, as well as coloring books on topics involving history, geography, art, and foreign language, historical paper dolls, and books with mazes, dot-to-dots, and hidden pictures for all ages.

Once we've found authors our children like, amazon.com or abe.com can be helpful resources for finding more of their books. If we feel the need, we can also use a textbook as a guide to what topics we should be covering. In many states, the school district is required to supply us with their textbooks if we request them, and we can glance over them to see exactly what our child is expected to learn in each subject for the year. Our own lack of education or fear of authority need not hold us back from providing a more relaxed and exciting style of homeschooling for our children.

Reading more about relaxed homeschooling and unschooling may also prove beneficial. John Holt, the father of unschooling, wrote many books, including *How Children Learn* and *Learning All the Time*, which provide some of the theories on which unschooling is based. Suzie Andres' *Homeschooling with Gentleness* draws greatly on the work of John Holt and proves that unschooling is not contrary to our Catholic faith; it also includes a lengthy booklist in the back. Gregory and Marine Millman's excellent *Homeschooling: A Family's Journey* tells the story of a Catholic family which uses an eclectic approach—a mix of conventional and unconventional educational methods—while sharing the wisdom about children and about life that they picked up along the way. Mary Hood's *The Joyful Homeschooler*, which is, unhappily, no longer in print, reveals very pragmatic reasons and methods for relaxed homeschooling from a Christian perspective, while *Christian Unschooling* provides some practical examples. John Taylor Gatto's *Weapons of Mass Instruction* will help us understand better the problems inherent in conventional schools and will inspire us to avoid similar pitfalls in our homeschool. Karen Andreola's *Charlotte Mason Companion* is an excellent introduction to Charlotte Mason's educational methods, including her ideas on living books and narration, while Clay and Sally Clarkson's *Educating the Wholehearted Child* shows us how to integrate learning into every day life. Further, *Mater et Magistra* is a wonderful, quarterly, Catholic homeschooling online magazine that features articles on all styles of homeschooling and incorporating our faith into our families' lives. Some, or all, of these resources can build our confidence in our own ability and in our children's ability to turn our house into a place where learning is a natural part of living.

If homeschooling mothers needed to possess heroic sanctity, superb organizational skills, and photographic memories, few, if any, could take on the job. Rather, homeschooling is our path to achieve sanctity, organization, and time management skills, and possibly even a better education than we previously experienced. Homeschooling doesn't require anything but that we love our children and we're committed to providing them with the best intellectual and spiritual formation we can.

# 11

## COMPARISONS

*"Comparisons are odorous."*
—WILLIAM SHAKESPEARE

COMPARING ourselves to others is usually, as Shakespeare says, odorous. Too many mothers feel discouraged or inferior for not doing all the things other homeschooling families are doing. Mothers suffering from chronic illness, or who have young children to care for, or who are burdened by financial concerns, may feel guilty for not providing the field trips or extracurricular activities that their friends manage for their children. Some mothers may feel inadequate because they don't do elaborate crafts or science projects like those featured in homeschooling magazines. Others may envy another mother's lively conversations with her children on history or literature. When we see or read about other parents passing on to their children their culinary or carpentry skills or their love of music or science or beekeeping, we may unconsciously compare ourselves with them and find ourselves woefully inferior. Even reading a homeschooling book like this may make some women feel discouraged, because they can't possibly follow all of the suggestions made.

Such comparisons produce no good fruit. Every home-schooling mother has a particular set of talents, interests, and assets that she can share with her children. Obviously, no mother will possess every skill or interest conceivably useful to her children; however, by sharing the skills and interests she does have, she'll be giving her children the confidence and experience to tackle the skills they need as they grow. We should remember, too, that God did not give our children to us blindly or randomly. He chose us, with our particular set of interests and abilities, to be the mother of our particular children with their particular needs and aspirations. We are not inadequate to raise and educate our children. With His help, we can provide what they need.

A few library books, some inexpensive, basic materials, and lots of encouragement often will make up for whatever is lacking in our experience or skills. Frequent field trips, fancy crafts, or science kits are not necessary. Expensive equipment is not necessary. Children will develop more creativity and problem-solving skills if they have simpler, more basic material to work with. In some situations, our lack of knowledge may also prove an advantage because our children will have to experiment and learn things for themselves, which will cultivate greater self-confidence, self-esteem, and pride of accomplishment. Moreover, we need to remember that the multitude of suggestions in homeschooling books are not meant to be followed in entirety, but are designed to provide a variety of ideas from which to choose, according to our needs and tastes.

Sometimes, if we feel strongly about our children learning something we know little about, we can learn with them. Our enthusiasm as we discover whittling techniques or literary classics may be contagious, and our children will often "catch" our enthusiasm. Other times, we may allow—or even require—our children to learn things we never learned. Even if we have no culinary expertise to pass on to our children, we can allow older children to try new recipes, as long as they understand safety rules. We could even require older children to take turns planning and preparing one dinner every week. Of course, we may have to learn something about cooking along the way, whether in listening to our child's chatter about his latest masterpiece or helping him figure out what went awry in his last attempt. We often learn more while homeschooling than we expect!

However, we have to accept that our children won't learn everything. They don't need to. We must realistically evaluate our own resources, decide on our priorities, and stop second-guessing our own decisions. Gardening is a good example, because it combines science, nutrition, and economics with useful life skills and thus looms as a large "should" for homeschooling mothers. Yet, for urban families, apartment dwellers, or renters, teaching our children to garden may be an impossible ideal, while to those with no prior experience or green thumb, gardening may seem like an intimidating and expensive gamble. Urban families may consider whether they have the space for an indoor or porch plant, or the money to rent gardening space nearby; suburban homeowners must decide if the educational benefits are worth the time and money necessary to begin a small garden in their yard. If we decide that gardening is not the best option for our family right now, then there is no need to feel guilty or inferior when we hear of others' gardens. If we do decide to invest in some sort of garden, whether in our own yard or elsewhere, we mustn't regret the time normally spent on other activities that is now being swallowed up by the garden; we have decided that this is a priority, and as such, it will usurp a good deal of time. This doesn't mean our focus will never change. We may spend a year or two establishing a vegetable garden and neglecting other extracurricular skills, and then, as our family's needs and interests change, we may spend less time on maintaining the garden while we devote our time to collecting prints of great works of art or learning to sing in harmony, or studying the life cycle of our pet frog. This isn't a lack of perseverance; it's providing breadth to our children's education.

Whatever our situation, whether our time and energy are depleted by chronic illness, frequent pregnancies, or part-time employment, or whether a lack of money or experience leads us to feel inadequate to deal with for our children's inquisitive minds, we can be sure God has given us what we need to raise and educate our children. Despite our own perceived deficiencies, we can still provide all of the benefits of homeschooling to our children: a loving, nurturing environment; the freedom to learn at their own pace and in their own way; plenty of time to pursue their own interests and develop creativity; protection from peer pressure; stronger family unity; and a daily habit of prayer which will foster a deeper understanding of our faith and love of God. Whatever our situation, these are things that, with God's merciful assistance, we can provide for our children, and these make up the most precious inheritance of all. The rest are extras, meant to supplement our homeschool or make homeschooling easier, more varied, or more fun; ultimately, they are completely unnecessary. Our homeschool does not need to look like the photos in a homeschooling magazine, or even like our friend's homeschool. All we need to homeschool our children, we already have: love. That will give our children the best possible start in life they could ever have.

# 12

## HUMILITY AND PATIENCE

*"Restraining my patience cost me so much*
*that I was bathed in perspiration."*

—ST. THERESE OF LISIEUX

THE combination of humility and patience together forms a sweet temper that is pleasant to be with and easy to learn from. As mothers, we must strive to daily become more humble and more patient. Moreover, humility and patience are intimately connected, for one who is humble does not expect everything to work according to his will and is less likely to become enraged when things go awry.

We homeschooling mothers have plenty of occasions to learn humility. When we have so much on our minds, so many responsibilities, we tend to forget a lot of little things—only to be reminded or corrected by our children. Obviously, we must make sure that these reminders or corrections are spoken respectfully; nevertheless, we may feel humbled when our children remember what we were supposed to remember! Busy as we are with so many little

85

tasks throughout each day, we often hurry and thus make more mistakes—be it bumping into a hapless toddler or spilling the milk we're pouring. To make matters more frustrating, when we mothers show our human frailty in any way, we have an audience of wide eyes watching us and ready to comment on our mistakes.

These occasions are salutary for our pride. As mothers and homeschoolers, we are the queens of our household, making most day-to-day decisions and solving a wide variety of problems. We decide what our family will eat, wear, and study, what crafts we will do, what music we'll hear, who will perform each chore, and what outside activities we'll participate in. We may allow our children to make some of these decisions, but they choose only by our sufferance, and we have veto power. Often our job involves resolving quarrels, affixing blame, correcting, and punishing; as a result, sometimes we can fall into a habit of superiority or condescension or impatience with our children. Thus, occasional humbling incidents may cure us of these tendencies, if we allow them to. Our own faults and forgetfulness can help us deal more sympathetically with the faults and forgetfulness of our children.

Homeschooling mothers have many opportunities to learn patience, as well. It is exasperating to exert time and energy teaching or correcting, only to have children not catch on through either inattention or contrariness, especially when faced with time limits or other constraints. Maybe the baby is crying and needs to eat, but we want to finish this lesson first, and our child is taking an unusually long time to answer our questions. We have so many responsibilities that we do a job hastily and then become annoyed when it becomes undone a minute later. We feel so much pressure and anxiety that our family and household live up to certain ideals that we become irate when the reality does not match up.

While we must not give up our ideals—we do want our children to clean up their rooms and do their work, for example—we must learn to accept whatever God sends us peacefully and deal with it appropriately. Getting angry with a child for a repeated fault, like failing to clean up his room, will rarely teach the child to overcome it. Sometimes we might take the child's disobedience personally, seeing the child's fault as a sign of a lack of respect or love for us. Other times, we may view a child's fault as a reflection of our own incompetence as a mother. Either way, we are seeing the child's fault through egocentric eyes. Of course, we don't mean to be selfish or egocentric; our emotions may be easily wounded because we have been hurt in the past, or we may have been trained to assess situations in terms of our own guilt. Nevertheless, we must work to conquer this preoccupation with ourselves. When we find ourselves overreacting or losing our temper, we must pause for a moment and ask, "Why is this particular incident so upsetting to me?" Once we realize that we are taking a child's disobedience personally, we realize how inappropriate our reaction is, and we can adjust our perspective. Then we can focus on accepting the situation that God has put us in, whether we like it or not, and deal with it more rationally.

As parents, our primary concern should be to address the needs of this child that God has given us. What does this child need? Apparently, he desperately needs to be trained, lovingly but firmly, to keep his room tidy. Once we have recognized our child's needs, then our minds can work on devising a system of rewards or deterrents that will effectively train our child to straighten his room regularly. Meanwhile, we learn to accept that we cannot control what faults our child has, and that his faults in no way reflect our own worth as mothers. What we can control is our reaction to his faults, and ideally our reaction will be whatever will most help this particular child overcome his faults and grow in virtue. When we strive to keep this perspective in mind, our child will receive the training he needs, and we will retain our inner peace; even more, we will be growing in patience and humility as we learn to trust and accept all that comes to us from the hand of God.

But for our daily little humiliations and annoyances to do us good, we must be open to God's grace. As always, we must take Christ as our Example. Although He was God, as man He "emptied himself, taking the form of a servant, being made in the likeness of men" (Philippians 2:7). He did not even demand what was His by nature. As a young Man, He was content to obey the commands of His mother and foster father, though He was their omniscient Creator and knew infinitely more than they did. During His public ministry, He befriended and lovingly trained twelve bickering, ignorant apostles who did not understand the suffering He would have to endure to redeem mankind. Further, He allowed Himself to be criticized by jealous, hypocritical Pharisees. During His Passion, He permitted Himself to be blindfolded and mocked by crude soldiers, and to be crucified as a criminal among thieves, taunted by some of the very souls He was dying to save. Never did He protest or proclaim His divinity to silence His maledictors. He performed miracles to confirm the faith of His followers, not to disprove His critics. Even today, He remains hidden on the altar, relying humbly on the reverence and good will of those who handle the Sacred Host. As St. Thomas Aquinas says, "Humility was extolled by Christ; and surely in this Sacrament He preaches an unrivalled humility, which disdains no dwelling, but consents to come like guest to any heart, even one that is defiled." If He Who is perfect set us an example through suffering all sorts of indignities, insults, and mockery, certainly we can learn to accept our little humiliations with patience and grace.

# 13

## TEACHING A CHILD TO READ

*"Fairy tales are not true—fairy tales are important, and they are not true, they are more than true. Not because they tell us that dragons exist, but because they tell us that dragons can be defeated."*

—G. K. CHESTERTON

FEW phases of homeschooling require as much patience as teaching a child to read, yet few are so rewarding. Listening to a child slowly and painstakingly sound out each word, often saying it incorrectly several times before getting it right, can be exasperating. Sometimes we literally have to bite our tongues to prevent ourselves from telling the child what the word is. If only the English language had a simpler, more consistent, system of phonetic rules! Then at least we wouldn't know the frustration of dinning a phonics rule into a child's head day after day only to watch him puzzle over a word that doesn't follow that rule.

However trying this stage may be, it is also one of the most rewarding. The pride and exhilaration on a child's face when he has read his first word, then his first sentence, and finally his first book, warms our hearts and makes all of those tongue-biting moments seem worth while. Moreover, as the child graduates to chapter books, a whole new world opens up for him. Anytime he is bored or tired or curious, he can pick up a book and find plenty to fill his mind and occupy his thoughts. We can enjoy sharing our own childhood favorites and watch his eyes moving across the page, frowning intently, or smiling delightedly, and sometimes even gasping or laughing out loud at what he is reading.

If a child expresses little interest in learning to read, or if he struggles unduly, then we must be careful not to force him to learn to read before he is ready. Relatives or friends may criticize us or look askance if our child isn't reading by a certain magic age, but we must firmly and confidently tell them that we as parents know best. Many a child has struggled for years to learn to read and hated reading ever after—all because he was compelled to read before he was ready. There is no magic age at which all children master rolling over, standing up, walking, or talking, and there is no correct age for all children to master reading. A late reader is not less intelligent or in greater danger of falling behind academically any more than a late walker is. The worst consequence of reading late is likely to be embarrassment or anxiety in the parent, or perhaps feelings of inferiority in the child if we pass our embarrassment and anxiety onto him. Generally, when a child learns to read later than usual, he catches up to the reading level of his peers in a matter of months. In fact, some homeschoolers feel that children do better if they learn to read when they are older than the age accepted in our nation's schools; for example, see the Millmans' *Homeschooling: A Family's Journey* or Raymond Moore's *Better Late Than Early*.

While teaching phonetic rules and helping a child sound out words is normally the most effective way to teach a child to read, we should be aware that some children do not learn to read this way. Some children actually learn to read by what is called "sight reading" or memorizing the look of every word. When schools try to teach all students to read by "sight reading," the results are disastrous, due to obvious drawbacks to this method—for one thing, it takes longer to memorize the spelling of every word than to learn a few rules about sounding words out, and children who learn this way have difficulty learning new words later. However, there are some children who learn to read more easily by sight reading, and though we can still teach them the basic rules of phonics, we should not try to force these children to learn to read in a way that is contrary to their learning style. If our child is learning to read, then we should be pleased with his progress and give him whatever assistance he needs to accomplish this feat in his own way.

We can encourage a child to want to read by reading books to him often so he can experience the joy and excitement books can bring. We should also frequently read books ourselves in front of our child to demonstrate that we really think reading is enjoyable, too; it's not just kids' stuff or school stuff; it's a tool for entertaining and informing oneself throughout life.

Once reading skills have been mastered, most children will naturally enjoy reading if they do not have too much access to television, videogames, or other electronic toys that induce intellectual passivity and laziness. For reluctant readers, a prescribed period of reading every day may be helpful, especially if the child is allowed to choose the book, subject to our own approval. Even if the book is below what we consider his reading level, the child will eventually desire to read harder books if he experiences enjoyment reading easy readers or picture books now.

Through frequent visits to local libraries and used book sales (see booksalefinder.com), we can surround our children with lots of good books in a variety of genres and topics to pique their curiosity and expand their interests. We must be aware, however, that many books purportedly written for young people in the last forty years may, in fact, be grossly inappropriate for youngsters. If we have any doubts, we should read the book first, and then consider whether the book is suitable. Are the children in the book punished when they disobey their parents or treat others unkindly? Do they keep important secrets from their parents? Do the characters in the book ridicule older people? Does the book treat family life respectfully, as a positive thing? Some bickering between fictional siblings is normal, but ultimately the love between siblings should be affirmed and the relationship presented as a positive thing. Does the storyline glorify pre-teen dating or romance? Does the girl fall for a charming, smooth-talking playboy or scoundrel who unrealistically changes his ways out of love for her?

Does the book portray unwholesome or abusive romantic relationships? Contain bad language? Focus on private bodily functions or discuss the body in a vulgar way? For example, some modern books frighten young girls by portraying the monthly period as extremely painful or inconvenient; not only is such a topic is too private for casual reading, but the perspective offered by the book may cast a shadow on a girl's image of her own sexuality and her wondrous ability to bring life into the world. Regarding historical fiction, we may want to have a reliable Catholic history book on hand so we can tell if the book is written with an anti-Catholic slant. Anne Carroll's *Christ the King, Lord of History* and *Christ and the Americas* are two excellent references that can help us sift through historical facts and fancies.

Not only should we do our best to ensure the books we provide are morally unobjectionable, they should also be well-written, high quality books. Many popular mystery series may be morally acceptable but consist of a-thrill-a-minute plots, which are highly improbable and may spoil the reader's appetite for less shallow, more realistic stories. Often recent books are simply not written well. While reading such books occasionally may not do any harm, a steady diet of low quality books is not ideal and may make it harder for our children to appreciate better books, which take more effort to read.

The benefits of reading are so numerous that we cannot hope to list them all here. Prolific reading is the best way to expand one's vocabulary, absorb the rules of grammar and spelling, and develop a polished writing style. Sometimes a reader can help a child learn to read; *Little Angel* by Linda Bromeier is an appealing new Catholic series that goes through all the phonetic rules one by one. But if a child does not enjoy readers, we can certainly find some very easy books to start him off with. Once a child has learned to read, we can throw away our readers, grammar texts, and spelling lists and invest in classics for all ages:

*Pirate's Promise* by Clyde Robert Bulla
*B Is for Betsy* by Carolyn Haywood
*All-of-a-Kind Family* by Sydney Taylor
*The Littles* by John Peterson
*Basil of Baker Street* by Eve Titus
*The Happy Little Family* by Rebecca Caudhill
*Little House on the Prairie* by Laura Ingalls Wilder
*The Apple and the Arrow* by Mary and Conrad Buff
*Heidi* by Johanna Spyri
*John Treegate's Musket* by Leonard Wibberly
*The Secret Language* by Ursula Nordstrom
*The Story of Doctor Dolittle* by Hugh Lofting
*Misty of Chincoteague* by Marguerite Henry
*Tom Playfair* by Fr. Francis Finn
*Madeleine Takes Command* by Ethel Brill
*Red Hugh, Prince of Donegal* by Robert T. Reilly
*The Magic Summer* by Noel Streatfeild
*The Phantom Tollbooth* by Norton Juster
*Pollyanna* by Eleanor H. Porter
*Homer Price* by Robert McCloskey

*Understood Betsy* by Dorothy Canfield

*Danny Dunn and the Homework Machine* by Jay Williams and Raymond Abrashkin

*Caddie Woodlawn* by Carol Ryrie Brink

*Half Magic* by Edward Eager

*A Little Princess* by Frances Hodgson Burnett

*Kidnapped* by Robert Louis Stevenson

*Little Women* by Louisa May Alcott

*If All the Swords in England* by Barbara Willard

*Anne of Green Gables* by L. M. Montgomery

*Crystal Snowstorm* by Meriol Trevor

*The Outlaws of Ravenhurst* by Sister M. Imelda Wallace

*The Adventures of Sherlock Holmes* by Sir Arthur Conan Doyle

*Lassie-Come-Home* by Eric Knight

*The Witch of Blackbird Pond* by Elizabeth George Speare

*El Cid, God's Own Champion* by James Fitzhenry

*They Loved to Laugh* by Kathryn Worth

*Lad: A Dog* by Albert Terhune

*The Last of the Mohicans* by James Fennimore Cooper

*Pride and Prejudice* by Jane Austen

*Ivanhoe* by Sir Walter Scott

*The Edge of Time* by Loula Grace Erdman

*Men of Iron* by Howard Pyle

*The Moonstone* by Wilkie Collins

*Daddy Long Legs* by Jean Webster

*Mutiny on the Bounty* by Nordhoff and Hall

*The Prisoner of Zenda* by Anthony Hope

*The Scarlet Pimpernel* by Baroness Orczy
*The Virginian* by Owen Wister
*Jane Eyre* by Charlotte Bronte
*Beau Geste* by P. C. Wren
*Middlemarch* by George Eliot
*Northwest Passage* by Kenneth Roberts
*Uncle Tom's Cabin* by Harriet Beecher Stowe
*A Tale of Two Cities* by Charles Dickens
*20,000 Leagues Under the Sea* by Jules Verne

. . . And so many more. Biographies of famous people, especially the saints, will provide further insights into history and religion that will also fascinate children. These are the books that will teach your child not only vocabulary and writing skills, but will open their minds to experiences and points of view they've never known, and introduce them to people and places and times they otherwise might never have met. Reading classics will show them in concrete ways the entrancing beauty of truth and virtue and the horrible consequences of evil and vice. Reading will ignite their imaginations and inspire them to think, to dream, and to write. Reading will show them that virtue is not only good, but admirable and lovable. Furthermore, reading good books will become a habit that can comfort, entertain, inform, and inspire them for the rest of their lives.

If children are exposed to lots of good quality literature during their formative years, separate spelling and grammar lessons are superfluous. Just as our children learned to speak grammatically by hearing us do so, they will learn to spell correctly and write grammatically by reading good books. It may take longer to learn spelling and punctuation this way, but the lessons will be more deeply ingrained, and the whole family will be spared the stress of two extra subjects to study. If we do find that a child is not learning spelling and punctuation as quickly as we would like, we can use a more natural, integrative approach by gently pointing out the errors in his assigned writing. While covering a child's creative writing with corrections can discourage creativity, we can pick out the most important or most common mistakes, especially those which actually make the writing hard to follow, and have our child correct them. If there are many spelling errors, rather than have the child fill his paper with erasures, he can practice the misspelled words on another sheet. Correcting their own spelling and punctuation errors lets children see clearly how spelling and punctuation are relevant to their life and needs; these are words that he uses and rules he needs to know to be able to communicate his ideas.

As the child grows older, perhaps fifth or sixth grade, we may want to teach him briefly whatever grammar he has not picked up already. One fun but thorough summary of English grammar is *Painless Grammar* by Rebecca S. Elliott, which can serve as a review and reference book for all the writers in our home. Because of our child's steady diet of good reading and his familiarity with writing, these rules will usually be fairly easy for him to master at that point. We may also want to have a good child's dictionary, thesaurus, and perhaps even a rhyming dictionary to assist our budding writers. With these resources, along with good reading habits, we can eliminate the need for unnecessary and tedious grammar and spelling lessons in our homeschool.

Surely, when we consider the lifelong rewards of reading, we will be careful to cultivate this habit in our children—patiently reading the same picture books to him over and over again; patiently waiting for our child to express interest in reading; patiently waiting for him to sound out each word; patiently explaining the inconsistencies in our English language; and joyfully watching the excitement grow in his eyes as the world of books opens up to him.

# 14

## TEACHING A CHILD TO WRITE

*"Writing badly anyone can understand who*
*writes at all; I for one do it perpetually."*

—G. K. CHESTERTON

TEACHING our children to write can be overwhelming to homeschooling parents, especially if we don't like to write ourselves. Some children, especially those who struggle with spelling or penmanship, may find writing a tedious struggle, but many children who are creatively inclined will enjoy this opportunity to express themselves. We must do our best to encourage both, particularly by allowing children to write about whatever topic they choose. While there are many good methods to teach children how to write, below is a summary of one simple way that doesn't require buying a lot of complicated curricula.

When our children are young, we can have them write a paragraph a week on whatever they want—something they've done recently, their favorite sports team, their chores, their last trip to the playground or grocery store, a field trip, or how they lost their last tooth. Here they can practice using introductory sentences and closing sentences to summarize what they're trying to say. Occasionally—perhaps once a month—we could have them fill out a book report, summarizing the story or describing their favorite scene or character. We can encourage them to write stories as well, or a regular family newspaper, including family news, trivia questions, and articles on whatever topic interests them.

As our children grow older, we can teach them to write research papers, usually one or two a year. They should learn to take notes on the information they gather so they won't be tempted to copy exact phrases or sentences from their resources. Starting each assignment with an introductory paragraph and ending with a closing paragraph, and making sure each paragraph is on a specific topic or aspect of the main topic, is crucial to good writing. Using an outline while planning the paper is another skill that can be learned at this time and will help the child keep to one topic per paragraph. If the child can choose the subject for his research paper, he will be much less reluctant to write it; also, the more the child writes, the easier it will become for him.

In junior high, we can have children start writing descriptive paragraphs in which they use as many senses as possible to vividly describe a particular place they've been. This is a good time for them to learn to use similes, metaphors, and alliteration. Once they have mastered descriptive writing, we can go on to comparison/contrast papers and then persuasive papers, now emphasizing that their opening paragraph must not only summarize what is to come, but pique the interest of the reader with dramatic phrases, while the closing paragraph should not only serve to recapitulate our main points, but also provide a fitting emotional climax to the paper.

High school is a great time to return to the literary analysis that we began with book reports in grade school. Comparing and contrasting similar books is an easy way to start, but even more satisfying is trying to discover what point the author was attempting to make in the novel, keeping in mind that not all novels will have a moral lesson as a theme. Examples from the text, including an occasional quote, will assist our teens in proving their thesis statement, which should be stated clearly in the opening paragraph. In addition, an occasional research paper, perhaps one or two a year, will enable the high schooler to further develop his ability to research, take notes, make an outline, choose the most important facts, and set them down on paper. Again, if the student can choose the topic, his interest in writing the paper will be much greater.

Of course, children of any age can be encouraged to write letters to relatives and friends, including thank you notes when they receive presents and get well notes for friends who are ill. Children of all ages can write poetry, too, without forgetting sonnets for the teenagers and humorous limericks for grade school children.

What we have outlined here is simply one plan that may assist us in teaching our children to write. There are other methods that different families may find more suited to their learning styles. This method is certainly not meant to limit a child who, for example, wants to write a persuasive paper in grade school; it is merely to ensure that every child has practiced each type of writing by the time he graduates. When we consider how essential effective communication is in every job and vocation—and how rare this skill is becoming in a social media-driven world—we must endeavor to do our best to encourage our children to voice their thoughts and feelings clearly, concisely, and effectively.

# 15

## DE-SCHOOLING

*"I learned the large Greek letters as I learnt
the large English letters, at home. I was told
about them merely for fun while I was still
a child; while the others I learnt during the
period of what is commonly called education,
that is, the period during which I was being
instructed by somebody I did not know, about
something I did not want to know."*

—G.K. CHESTERTON

WHEN we decide to take our child out of a conventional school and teach him at home, experts often recommend a transition time of de-schooling. This is basically a break from formal education, which allows the child to recover from his negative academic experiences, instead of merely transferring his resentment from his schoolteacher to his homeschooling mother. The general rule of thumb is to allow one month of de-schooling for every year the child has spent in school; however, as mothers, we are the best judges of when a child has overcome his negative attitudes and is refreshed enough to start anew.

Not all children removed from conventional schools will need a prolonged de-schooling period. How much de-schooling is necessary depends greatly on why the child was removed. If we removed the child because we had objections to the moral content of the material being taught, de-schooling won't be as critical; but if we felt our child was being pushed to learn material he wasn't ready for, or if our child was struggling due to a learning disability or a teaching method that conflicted with his learning style, then our child may need a few months' break before he can face academics with a healthy, curious, and relaxed attitude.

The temptation to skip or cut short this de-schooling phase can be strong. After taking the leap of faith in removing a child from a conventional school setting, we may feel pressured to prove to ourselves or to others that we can do just as well or better at home. We'll want to vindicate our decision by showing immediate progress. We must ask ourselves, however, are we more interested in long-term or short-term results? If we want long-term results, we may have to sacrifice some short-term improvement. Again, we know our children best. If we feel our child is ready to begin academics immediately and we have pressing reasons to avoid delay, we can begin relaxed lessons, but we should be sensitive to our child's feelings of low self-esteem or anxiety, which may be souvenirs of an unhappy classroom experience. If the anxiety does not abate within a few weeks, we must consider de-schooling for an extended time.

If possible, de-schooling should last until the child exhibits some interest in learning on his own. With no lessons, he'll have plenty of free time to develop hobbies and interests, and at some point he'll want to find books about his hobby, or to make measurements or calculations. If we're wise, we'll be there to assist him without pushing him. Slowly and patiently, we can watch our child realize that there is a reason to learn to read or to count or to add—that learning does have some relation to real life— and that learning can be fun.

Making lessons fun is not just something we do because we feel badly for children with hours of tedious homework to do. Making learning fun actually makes learning more effective. We remember information better when we use that information; if we find information relevant to our lives or interesting or somehow important, we make it our own, and it becomes part of us, and then we remember it—not just for a test, but for all of our lives.

This is the experience we are trying to create in our homeschool. But if a child has been nearly traumatized by a negative learning experience, it may be practically impossible for him to approach reading, writing, or math without tension and dread. We need to back off, allow healing to occur, and wait for the child to discover the joy of learning on his own.

De-schooling can be scary because we're not in control. But isn't that what motherhood is all about—surrendering control, little by little each day, to allow our children the freedom to learn through experience, make mistakes, and gradually assume control of their own lives?

De-schooling requires lots of trust. We must trust our own decision to homeschool and to de-school. We must trust our child's ability to heal and eventually come to value learning. We must trust that God made our child's mind to love and to grasp the truth.

De-schooling demands our patience and our love. Let us ask our child's guardian angel and patron saints to assist him in his recovery from negative academic experiences and in guiding him to use his mind to its fullest potential.

# 16

## DISCIPLINE

*"When a child is given to his parents, a crown is made for that child in Heaven, and woe to the parents who raise a child without consciousness of that eternal crown!"*

—ARCHBISHOP FULTON J. SHEEN

EVEN if we strive to create a relaxed, non-stressful learning environment for our children, our homeschool will not work if we don't enforce discipline. If our children speak to us disrespectfully, or if they disobey or neglect their chores, then we will accomplish very little, and the atmosphere in our house will not radiate the peace, love, and joy that the children need for a healthy formation—and that we need for our own mental and spiritual well-being. We must not take lightly our responsibility to raise our children to be saints. Sadly, since the fall of Adam and Eve, this requires discipline at times.

Our discipline must be calm, controlled, and firm. We must do our best to conquer our own temper, or our discipline will upset our children without teaching them.

We must have a few ideas for punishments on hand so we can assign a punishment right away. Scolding a child without giving a punishment will leave us feeling angry because justice has not been meted out, and it will teach our children that our words mean nothing. Disciplinary methods could include taking away a privilege, a toy, or a dessert; assigning a chore or some moderate exercise like ten sit-ups, according to the child's ability; requiring the child to write a paragraph on why he mustn't repeat his fault; or assigning an extra chore, such as sharpening all the pencils or doing dishes when it's not his turn. All of these punishments may serve as deterrents. Some children, particularly young children, respond best to corporal punishment, which should always be administered while we are calm. If a child has hurt another child, he should apologize, in addition to his punishment.

One of the most common infractions among children is fighting. There is truth in the old saying, "You can choose your friends but not your family," and we mustn't become too discouraged if we can't completely root it out. Nevertheless, we must work to create a peaceful, harmonious atmosphere in our house and to teach our children, as much as we can, to get along. If a child has been annoying his siblings purposely, we can send him to his room, or we can separate two children who keep bickering or fighting. Separation, however, is only a short-term solution and will not teach the children to get along with each other. Therefore, if two of our children consistently don't get along, we may want to consider requiring them to spend an hour together every day. Sometimes we can give the two bickering children something special, that they aren't usually allowed to have, while they play together. The novelty of a special toy can jumpstart their friendship. When children are forced to play together, they often learn to get along out of necessity. Moreover, spending time together can reveal qualities in each other that they never knew of or appreciated before. If two children keep bickering while playing separately, then we can tell them to play a certain game together as punishment—if it's not too long a game, we can have them play it over and over until they can get through a whole game without saying anything unpleasant to each other or hitting each other. We could also discipline two quarrelsome children by having them each write down seven or more good things about each other. (Such assignments can also provide humor years later.)

Treating others with patience and charity is the core of the Christian life, so we must do our best to prevent enmity from developing between siblings. Private conversation with each child may help also. We must validate each child's frustrations, acknowledging, for instance, that his little brother can be very irritating at times. Once we acknowledge the child's feelings, the child will feel that we are on his side, and he will listen more openly to what we have to say. We then can assure him that if he treats his brother or sister more kindly, then eventually the brother or sister will probably reciprocate and start behaving better towards him. We can help our child understand the underlying cause for the continual fighting. For example, if a child feels excluded by his siblings, he will be likely to retaliate by teasing or laughing at them, so his siblings need to include him, not in every game, but more often. If a child finds a sibling's boasting bothersome, we can explain that most children—and even adults—who boast do so because they feel somehow slighted and are trying to make themselves seem more important; they are not really trying to put others down, but endeavoring to raise themselves. Sometimes a child will find it easier to be patient with a sibling when he understands why his sibling is acting in a certain way.

Of course, our children should know that when they hurt others, they are hurting Jesus. We can explain this to our child by asking how he would feel if someone said, "I love you," to him and then ripped up a paper doll or paper soldier he just made. Would he really believe this person loved him? No, because if we love someone, we respect and care for what he has made and loves. Yet that is how we treat Jesus when we pray every day, "Jesus, I love You" and then hit a brother or sister whom He made and for whom He died.

Stories from the saints can also help us inculcate sibling charity and peace. We can tell our children about St. John Vianney, who, upon receiving a letter from another priest which criticized him, even to the point of saying he was not knowledgeable enough to hear confessions, humbly wrote back, "Most dear and most venerated confrere, what good reasons I have for loving you! You are the only person who really knows me." St. John went on to ask his fellow priest to write to the bishop with his complaints so that he could be removed from a position for which he felt he was unworthy. If our children would imitate this example even a little, so that when a sibling criticizes them they hasten to say, "Oh, I'm sorry I upset you. That was thoughtless of me," they'll be surprised at how quickly their critic's anger is diffused. Often he will even start apologizing to them.

Treating each other with respect and not assuming the worst is crucial for our children to get along with each other. St. Thomas Aquinas can teach our children this kind of respect. Once, as a seminarian, he was absorbed in study, and his classmates thought it would be funny to tell him there was a flying ox outside the window. Hearing this, Thomas ran to the window to see. When his fellow seminarians laughed at him, asking, "How could you believe that there was a flying ox?" he replied wisely, "I would rather believe that an ox could fly than that a Dominican would tell a lie." Needless to say, the laughter ceased. Our children need to give each other the benefit of the doubt, and not assume the worst when others annoy or tease them, just as St. Thomas did.

Above all, we should impress upon our child's mind that these daily, little battles are the stuff of which sanctity is made. It is in the small acts of self-denial, when we bite back unkind words or restrain the impulse to annoy, jeer, or hit, that we will truly become saints. We can remind our children of Christ, Who bore the ridicule and cruelty of the soldiers. We can tell our children about the saints, who rejoiced to suffer for Our Lord. We can point out that suffering these daily little trials with fortitude is the best preparation for more serious trials to come, when, as adults, our children may have to sacrifice respect, comfort, a promotion, a raise in pay, or some other worldly good, for the sake of Christ. How will our children bear the sneers and scorn of others as adults when they don't laugh at immoral jokes at a meeting, or cooperate in dishonest business deals at the office, or condone abortion or sterilization at the hospital, or participate in some other activity that is contrary to their faith, if they cannot bear the teasing of their brothers and sisters at home? How can they be prepared to suffer persecution for Christ in the world if they cannot endure the irritations of family life? This ideal of Christian love and heroism must be the guiding force behind all our discipline, for while punishment provides short-term deterrence, Christian ideals provide life-long inspiration.

Discipline is never a fun thing to think about or to do. The good news is that the more consistently we discipline, the less we'll have to discipline. Once we establish a pattern of respect, obedience, order, and harmony, infractions will become the exception, not the norm. Deeds must have consequences, or our children will fall into bad habits, habits that will grow harder and harder to break as they grow older, enslaving their wills and draining them of inner peace. Therefore, if we truly love our children and want what is best for them, we must discipline them—lovingly but firmly. Let us, therefore, imitate our Father in heaven, for "whom the Lord loveth, he chastiseth" (Proverbs 3:12).

# 17

## TEACHING RELIGION

*"A scrap of knowledge about sublime things is
worth more than any amount of trivialities."*

—ST. THOMAS AQUINAS

HOMESCHOOLING allows us tremendous scope
and flexibility in teaching our faith to our children,
and religion textbooks are only one of the myriad tools and
methods for us to use to pass on the truths of our faith.

For instance, celebrating the liturgical year in our
home teaches the children so much about their faith without their ever realizing that they are learning.

In Advent, a Jesse Tree can teach our children about
all the most important Old Testament figures, as we
make ornaments symbolizing each character and read the
appropriate story from a children's Bible, such as *The New
Catholic Picture Bible* by Fr. Lovasik. Older children can
also try to determine how each Old Testament character
prefigures Christ, and can read the major prophecies con-
cerning the Savior. As we prepare for Christ's birth with
little acts of self-giving, we can remind our children that

we are also preparing ourselves for Christ's second coming, when He shall come as Judge. Many families allow the children to place a piece of straw or yarn into the manger for each good deed or sacrifice they've done during the day; this drives home very clearly the truth that Christ taught when He said, "As long as you did it to one of these, my least brethren, you did it to me" (Matthew 25:40).

During the Christmas season, we can read about the Savior's birth and discuss why He became man. Singing Christmas carols and then explaining their meaning can be fruitful, particularly with those carols that are rich in symbolism, such as "We Three Kings."

Lent is a perfect time to introduce mortification, self-sacrifice, alms-giving, and spiritual reading, especially meditating on the Passion of Christ. We can take our children to the Stations of the Cross at our parish or pray the Stations at home as a family. We can discuss why Christ died for our sins. Holy Thursday will provide an opportunity to review our children's knowledge of the Mass: do they remember that the Mass is the same sacrifice as Christ dying on the cross at Calvary, presented in an unbloody manner? Do they understand the meaning of the term the "Real Presence"? Have they considered why Christ instituted this holy sacrament?

With Good Friday and Easter Sunday, we can naturally discuss the very core of our faith—Christ's death, redemption, and resurrection—and how we know that Christ is divine. We can ask our children why the egg and the butterfly are symbols of the resurrection. (Like Christ's tomb, the egg does not appear to contain life—it looks like an inanimate oval rock until it hatches and out comes a fluffy chick. Similarly, a caterpillar's cocoon appears to be dead matter until the butterfly emerges.)

On Divine Mercy Sunday we can pray the Divine Mercy Chaplet and talk about the visions of St. Faustina.

Pentecost is the time for a little ecclesiastic theology—it's the birthday of the Church, the Bride and the Mystical Body of Christ. Pentecost is also the time for a litany or novena to the Holy Spirit and a discussion of the sacrament of Confirmation.

In May, we can sing hymns to Our Lady and then explain some of those mysterious terms, like "immaculate," "advocate," and "mediatrix."

On Corpus Christi, we can review our children's understanding of the Real Presence and go over the parts of the Mass which we may have been too busy to discuss in detail on Holy Thursday.

In June we focus on the Sacred Heart and Christ's infinite love for us. We can explain what "reparation" means and make some acts of reparation as a family or consecrate our family to the Sacred Heart. Perhaps we could even read a loud Mary Fabyan Windeatt's biography of St. Margaret Mary or some other book on the Sacred Heart every evening.

Ordinary time can be used to go over the miracles and preaching of Christ's public life. We can discuss the Gospel reading after Mass or read a little bit from the Gospels every evening as a family. Alternately, reading a brief life of the saint of the day throughout the year not only familiarizes the children with the saints, but also offers real models of holiness and even teaches an occasional lesson on doctrine.

In October we emphasize the rosary, which helps us meditate on the entire life of Christ. We can also read a good book about the apparitions at Fatima, which are particularly fascinating to children because the events at Fatima happened to young children.

Finally, in November, we pray for the souls in Purgatory and meditate on our own encounter with death and judgment. We can take this opportunity to explain to our children the difference between our own particular judgment and the general judgment that will come at the end of the world.

Hymns after morning prayers that correspond to the liturgical season or other prayers and novenas that relate to the liturgical year teach our children a tremendous amount about the faith just in the course of every day life. We can occasionally add appropriate crafts or activities, like making saint statues out of clothespins for All Saints' Day, or writing poems about Easter or Pentecost, or performing little skits about the life of the children's patron saints on the appropriate feast days. Such activities will make the various liturgical seasons and feasts even more fun and memorable. We can also look online for famous paintings of the life of Christ or of favorite saints, and print them out on a color printer at the library for a small fee, and display them in our house on the appropriate day. Many children love receiving holy cards or coloring books about Christmas,

Easter, or the saints. So much can be learned just by living the faith each day!

This is not to say that there is not room for religion textbooks at all. *Chats With God's Little Ones* is a lovely book published by Lepanto Press to teach children in kindergarten or first grade about their basic prayers and doctrine. *The Baltimore Catechism*, published in three levels by the Catholic Book Publishing Company, features the traditional question-and-answer format, accompanied by beautiful illustrations and helpful diagrams. The first *Baltimore Catechism* is particularly useful for preparation for First Holy Communion; the questions and answers are, for the most part, so basic and concise that most children would benefit from memorizing them, whereas the two older books have much longer and more complicated answers which are more important to understand than memorize. The *Image of God* books, a new series published by Ignatius Press, and *Our Holy Faith*, an older series reprinted by Neumann Press, are both known for their solid orthodox content. For high schoolers, TAN Books reprints the theologically solid religion series by Fr. John Laux, or we could look into the shorter *Catholicism* series, put out by CR Publications. Different series of texts will appeal to different learning styles and tastes.

But we certainly don't need to stick to textbooks all of the time, especially if our children find them dull or repetitive. There are so many other resources available to teach children the Catholic faith. The old Arch Books and the Alice in Bibleland books are two series that are out of print, but still pretty easy to find online or at used books sales, and both teach children Bible stories with a rhyming text and colorful illustrations, perfect for pre-schoolers through the primary grades. (Just beware of the rare Protestant bias in the text.) *The Treasure Box* books from TAN are a gorgeous choice for young ones. The Angel Food books from Neumann Press or *The First Christians, St. Patrick's Summer,* or any of Marigold Hunt's other books, republished by Sophia Press, are informative and superbly written for grade schoolers. An attractive child's Catholic Bible is appropriate for any age. A wonderful, recently reissued CD, *24 Catholic Songs for Children,* along with a matching coloring cook, is available from JoyfulCatholic.com. This CD reinforces traditional catechism questions with cheerful but reverent songs.

Occasionally biographies of saints can substitute for religious instruction. The Vision books, reprinted by Ignatius Press, or the excellent biographies by Mary Fabyan Windeatt, reprinted by TAN Books, are two edifying and enjoyable series for fourth grade to adult readers. For more ideas on sharing the faith with our children, we can look for *We and Our Children* (republished by Sophia Press as *How to Raise Good Catholic Children*), *The Year and Our Children* (also published by Sophia), and *The Saints and Our Children* (reprinted by TAN). All of these are filled with beautiful, practical gems by Catholic mother Mary Reed Newland.

Spiritual reading can sometimes serve as religion class as well. Now, before giving a child any spiritual reading book, we should always consider if our child is prone to spiritual scruples, and if this book may cause a scrupulous person more harm than good. Junior high school students and older will learn the basics of the spiritual life from *Seventeen Steps to Heaven* by Leo Trese, *The Sinner's Guide* by Ven. Louis Grenada, *Think Well On It* by Fr. Richard Challoner, or *Preparation for Death* by St. Alphonsus Liguori. Scott Hahn's *The Lamb's Supper* will enhance their appreciation for the Mass.

Aside from saint biographies and spiritual reading, there are innumerable living books on Catholicism. If we can find an out-of-print copy of Fr. Albert Shamon's *Treasure Untold*, or Fr. Ronald Knox's *The Creed in Slow Motion*, our high schoolers will appreciate the skillful blend of doctrine, spirituality, and humor while plumbing the depths of the Apostles' Creed. High schoolers will benefit on many levels from reading the spiritual classics, such as *Introduction to the Devout Life* by St. Francis de Sales, *The Little Catechism of the Cure of Ars* by St. John Vianney, or *The Story of a Soul* by St. Therese of Lisieux. *Why Does God Permit Evil?* by Dom Bruno Webb is a lesser known classic that can strengthen the faith while provoking interesting discussions for high schoolers. Our teens' understanding and appreciation of Holy Scripture would be greatly enriched by reading Bishop Frederick Justus Knecht's superb *A Practical Commentary on the Bible*, which explores the Bible historically, doctrinally, and spiritually; we could use this book to cover the Old Testament one year and the New Testament the next, or we could squeeze it into one year by having our teen read a chapter a day. *Conversation with Christ* by Peter Thomas Rohrbach will teach our young adults an easy method of mental prayer. Frank Sheed's *Map of Life*, Fulton J. Sheen's *Life of Christ*, Fr. Francis Ripley's *This Is the Faith*, St. Thomas Aquinas' *Shorter Summa*—there are so many fabulous books on our faith that we could keep listing them indefinitely. We may benefit immensely by reading some of these spiritual classics ourselves.

Of course, Church history should form part of every Catholic child's education, though most homeschoolers incorporate it into their history lessons, rather than religion. Anne Carroll's *Christ the King, Lord of History* and *Christ and the Americas* are popular among homeschooling parents and students alike because of their exciting style and their Catholic perspective on history. Thomas E. Woods Jr.'s books are also highly recommended, particularly *How the Catholic Church Built Western Civilization*. Another excellent book which dispels many myths concocted by anti-Christian historians would be *Columbus and Cortez, Conquerors for Christ* by John Eidsmoe.

Teens especially want to know why we believe, and we can satiate this yearning with apologetics. We can start with the incredibly easy to read *Yes Or No* by Peter Kreeft (and later tackle the much longer but equally engaging *Catholic Handbook of Apologetics* by Kreeft and Tacelli), both of which will help the reader learn, not only how to defend the faith, but also how to think logically and coherently. Fr. John O'Brien's *Faith of Millions* both explains and

defends Catholic beliefs in simple language. C. S. Lewis'
*Mere Christianity*, Scott and Kimberly Hahn's *Rome Sweet
Home*, and Chantal Epie's *The Scriptural Roots of Catholic
Teaching* are all thought-provoking, informative, yet readable, apologetics books. G. K. Chesterton's masterpiece,
*The Everlasting Man*, would provide a fitting climax of a
teen's religious education.

Textbooks can provide some structure or form the
foundation for our children's knowledge of the faith.
However, there are so many living books on the Catholic
faith that we may not need to use many religion textbooks
at all, considering that children learn best from real-life
experiences and from what Charlotte Mason called "living books" that truly engage their interest. Fortunately,
homeschooling allows ample opportunity to permeate our
homes with Catholic materials and liturgical observances,
so that children's religion will not be just another subject,
but an integral part of their lives.

# 18

## CULTURE

*"In touching the inner core of our beings
beautiful music ennobles and uplifts.
It possesses a persuasive power toward the
good, while coarse and barbaric music
cheapens, degrades, and promotes evil.
Handel's Messiah lifts the mind and
heart to the glories of the Incarnation and
Resurrection, while rock, not surprisingly,
is often accompanied by drugs and sexual
immorality—and at times is followed by a
riot. 'From their fruits you will know them.'"*

—FR. THOMAS DUBAY

AS mothers, we mold our children's characters and tastes, and our home will reflect our own culture and taste—which our children will absorb. We must, therefore, be very careful about the content and quality of anything we allow in our house. We must not allow others to dictate what is appropriate for our children. It doesn't matter what other parents are allowing their children to read, watch, or listen to. If a song, book, or movie does not uphold our Christian values, then we are obliged to forbid our children access to it. If it could be a temptation against chastity or cause desensitization to violence, then we must reject it. Some movie guides for children say, "For mature children only." Why? Are mature children less susceptible to temptation than immature children? Hardly. Mature children, after watching or reading something risqué or violent, may be less apt to make crude comments that embarrass us, but that doesn't mean that risqué or violent movies and books don't tempt them dangerously, even if they may be too embarrassed to tell us. Anything that could rob our children's souls of their innocence or tempt them to sin must not be allowed. Our children's immortal souls are at stake. In these impressionable years, we want our children to be growing in holiness; the last thing we should do is place obstacles in their path that will make them a slave to concupiscence.

If we are going to wage a battle against the immoral so-called "culture" of today's society, then we must provide our children with true culture that really entertains, uplifts, and edifies. First, we must stock our house with good quality music. Obviously, this should include some classical music, both instrumental and vocal, including opera and operetta. Children of all ages may particularly enjoy the lively music and humor of the operettas by Gilbert and Sullivan, particularly *The HMS Pinafore*, *The Pirates of Penzance*, and *The Mikado*. A songbook with the most popular songs from these operettas will allow us to sing along, so even the younger children can join in, while older children may enjoy reading the plays in their entirety. One bright and cheery adaptation of Gilbert and Sullivan songs for children is *I Have a Song to Sing, O!*, edited by John Langstaff. Gregorian chant or other Catholic hymns playing in the background during the day can also be uplifting and soothing; Icon Studio Productions' *Gregorian Chant for Kids* Teaching DVDs might be a fun way to teach children this traditional music, especially if we don't know it well ourselves. Folk songs from different countries, including American folk music, standards from the first half of the twentieth century, and songs from Broadway musicals are other resources for good quality music, though we still need to be vigilant about the words; modern music does not hold a monopoly on inappropriate lyrics! Barbershop music can be both catchy and appealing, and it may lead to our children trying to sing in harmony.

We should steer away from too many love songs, especially for younger children, and find songs about other topics:

- Songs about geographical places, such as "Mississippi Mud," "Carolina in the Morning," "California, Here I Come";

- Songs about music, such as "I Love a Piano" or "Won't You Play a Simple Melody";

- Polkas like "Hoop-de-doo" or "Papa, Won't You Dance With Me?";

- Cowboy songs like "Home on the Range" or "Don't Fence Me In";

- Songs that reinforce a positive attitude towards life, such as "Pick Yourself Up," "Look for the Silver Lining," "Accentuate the Positive," or "The Best Things in Life Are Free";

- Folk songs, like "Oh, Susannah" or "Pollywoddle Doodle."

If we have not chosen to throw out the TV, we can watch reruns of *The Lawrence Welk Show* on PBS, which feature a variety of genres of songs that children and adults may enjoy; we can also check out yestermusic.com, beautiful-music.com, or thehansonfamilysingers.com for music with innocent words and upbeat tunes that will be appropriate for the whole family. (This is not an endorsement of every product offered on these websites, but merely stating good music can be found there.) Although most popular songs today are love songs, popular songs of the past covered a variety of topics. Surely we can find some that are palatable to our children and ourselves.

An interest in music could spur some forays into history, as well. We can find biographies of the composers of classical music and of folk music, from Handel to Stephen Foster. *The Spiritual Lives of the Great Composers* by Patrick Kavanaugh, available from bywayofthefamily.com, reveals that many of the great classical composers were devout Christians whose faith inspired their work. Some patriotic songs have their origins from the Civil War, such as "Glory, Glory, Hallelujah" and "When Johnnie Comes Marching Home Again." Other songs, like "Till We Meet Again," "It's a Long Way to Tipperary," and "How Ya Gonna Keep 'Em Down on the Farm (After They've Seen Paree)" teach us a little about Americans' mentality during World War I. "Ain't We Got Fun!" and other songs from the 1920s reflect the defiant, carefree spirit of that age, while "I Haven't Time to Be a Millionaire" and "Pocketful of Dreams" were clearly penned during the Great Depression. "When the Lights Go On Again All Over the World," "Boogie Woogie Bugle Boy of Company B," and "There'll Be Bluebirds Over the White Cliffs of Dover" became popular during World War II. Music from different eras can bring history to life in our children's minds.

Before we choose music for our children—and ourselves—to listen to, we should be aware of some of the harmful effects of rock music, including rock n' roll, soft rock, hard rock, and rap. Although the scientific research on this subject is still scarce, there is some evidence that rock music does not constitute good quality, wholesome music, even if the lyrics are innocuous. Rock music focuses on the rhythm, not on the melody, which naturally makes it less melodious—and, therefore, less musical than most other kinds of music. While melodious music uplifts the listener by its intrinsic beauty, appealing to the intellect and the nobler emotions, the beat of rock music bypasses the intellect and appeals to the lower passions. Hard rock stirs up anger and unchaste desires, while soft rock tends to induce depression or melancholy. Both hard rock and soft rock have been found to foster incoherent thinking and a lack of concentration, encouraging our emotions to usurp the authority of our reason—the exact opposite of the effect of the baroque music of Mozart, Bach, and Vivaldi. Furthermore, the rhythm in rock music is contrary to the body's natural rhythm, which adversely affects the electrochemical synapses in the brain and also makes the music physically addictive. In his book, *Closing of the American Mind*, Allan Bloom compares the long-term effects of rock music on the mind to that of drugs. What a brilliant strategy of the devil to use our emotions to undermine our self-mastery through seemingly harmless songs, songs whose very beats have an addictive effect that few people will have the insight and motivation to resist!

There are several resources containing more information on the detrimental effects of rock music. Look for Dr. Arlene Taylor's article, "Music and the Mind: Potential Negative Impact" at arlenetaylor.org; Laurence O'Donell's "Music and the Brain" at cerebromente.org; and "The Effects of Music on the Brain" at angelfire.com. An intriguing experiment was reported in the article "Teen Proves Hard Rock's Bad for You" by Lorraine Eaton, which was published in the August 3, 1997, issue of *The Virginia Pilot*. This article describes the meticulous, award-winning experiments of high school student David Merrell, who timed three groups of mice finding their way through a maze and then exposed them to different kinds of music for ten hours a day, over a period of time, to see how the music would affect their ability to go through the maze. At first, the mice were able to navigate the maze in about ten minutes. The control group listened to no music, but through repetition over time, they were able to improve their scores by five minutes. The mice who listened to baroque music were able to improve their scores by eight and a half minutes. However, the mice who listened to hard rock took three times longer to get through the maze. Even more thought-provoking: Merrell kept all the mice in separate compartments, because an earlier experiment had to be cut short when the mice who had listened to hard rock killed each other. What does this experiment imply about the effect rock music could have on our children?

Music moves our emotions and touches our hearts; music forms an important backdrop to the events and decisions in our lives. Don't we want such a powerful influence to be a positive, uplifting one? An influence that will teach us to love beauty and purity, an influence that will foster noble thoughts and ideas? Although we may be attached to rock music because we grew up with it, we must question whether this is the type of influence we want to pass on to our children—and we may even want to consider its negative effects in our own lives.

With all of this in mind, we can look for free outdoor concerts sponsored by nearby towns during the summer, as well as free or inexpensive concerts held at some Christian churches in our area. These will greatly enhance our children's appreciation of music, as the experience of listening to music on a CD player in your home is totally different from watching someone perform right in front of you. Children who aren't exposed to lots of television will not find such concerts dull, as long as they are old enough to sit still for an hour or two. Since most free concerts take place on weekends or evenings, when most fathers are home from work, we could take only the children old enough to enjoy the concert while our husbands watch the little ones. Of course, if our husband works odd hours or lots of overtime, he may not be home to watch the younger ones, and we may have to try to bring everybody, or hire a babysitter for the occasion. The cost of a babysitter might prohibit us from doing this very often, but it could be worth it occasionally, especially since the cost of a babysitter will probably be less than the price of tickets to a more conventional concert.

Of course, music is not the only avenue for introducing culture into our homes. We may want to keep the television for carefully chosen DVDs or videos. Many older and more innocent TV shows and movies are now available in these forms, although we should preview them, as they may not always be as innocent as we remember. We can also find interesting documentaries or musical performances on video or DVD. The library is a good source here again. We can also find movies on the saints, such as the cartoon *Nicholas: The Boy Who Became Santa* and similar videos put out by CCC, which are available from most Catholic stores, or the old Warner Brothers' *The Miracle of Our Lady of Fatima* or *Joan of Arc* starring Ingrid Bergman. There are plenty more movies with religious themes, such as *Boystown*, *Come to the Stable*, or *Going My Way*, or the more modern but deeply moving *Facing the Giants*. Some non-religious movies can also provide inspiring role models for our children, such as *Mr. Smith Goes to Washington* or *You Can't Take It with You*, both starring Jimmy Stewart; *Mr. Deeds Goes to Town* or *Sergeant York*, both with Gary Cooper; *The Adventures of Robin Hood* starring Errol Flynn with Jimmy Stewart; or *Boomerang* with Dana Andrews.

We can also keep our eyes open for movies of books our children have read. Some of the better versions include *Anne of Green Gables* with Megan Follows; *The Prisoner of Zenda* and *A Tale of Two Cities*, starring Ronald Colman; *Little Women* with Katherine Hepburn (although the other versions aren't bad); *Pride and Prejudice* and *Wuthering Heights* with Laurence Olivier; *Ivanhoe* with Robert Taylor; *And Then There Were None* starring Barry Fitzgerald and Roland Young; *Jane Eyre* with Joan Fontaine; *The Picture of Dorian Gray* with George Sanders; *The Scarlet Pimpernel* with Leslie Howard; *Beau Geste* with Gary Cooper; Walt Disney's old *Treasure Island* and *Swiss Family Robinson*; and so forth. If possible, we really should try to have our children read the books before they watch the movies. They may even enjoy writing a report comparing and contrasting the two versions. For our high school biology students, Ben Stein's *Expelled* as a supplement can provide a humorous but thoughtful look at the claims of evolution.

Of course, one of the all-time favorite movies for Catholic families is the superb *The Sound of Music*, which can be enjoyed by all ages, over and over again. Other musicals, such as *In the Good Old Summertime, Holiday Inn, Top Hat, Showboat, Rose Marie, The King and I, First Love, Spring Parade,* or *State Fair* can not only entertain, but add to our children's music appreciation. To further encourage our children's interest in music, we can purchase the movie soundtrack or the sheet music of the songs from the movie if our children play an instrument. (Even the movies mentioned here should be previewed, as some have themes not suitable for younger children.)

We can look for rare movies like *Twelve Angry Men* with Henry Fonda or *The Caine Mutiny* with Humphrey Bogart, which may provoke thoughtful discussions for our teens. Soap opera-type movies, even if they are labeled "classics," should not be watched. Neither should movies with unrealistic love stories or stories with gravely flawed heroes and heroines. However, other movies, including musicals, comedies with no crude humor, religious, historical, or literary movies can entertain our family and teach our children that what is true, good, and beautiful is actually a lot of fun.

However, the TV is not necessary to inculcate a refined taste and culture in our children; it's one tool of many, and certainly not the best. It can be hard to find worthwhile movies, and it's even harder to limit the time spent in front of the TV to what we originally planned. Finding good movies is only one of many ways to introduce our children to true culture. If, after much thought and prayer, we have decided to throw away the television, we should not change our minds lightly; the harm done by too much watching far outweighs the good of the occasional worthwhile movie.

The primary avenue for culture will, of course, be books, as we've discussed at length. We must try to introduce our children to a variety of genres, including poetry of different kinds. Children's poetry is charming and often humorous, but children should also be exposed to narrative poetry, lyric poetry, limericks, and sonnets. The hilariously unconventional poetry of Ogden Nash will entertain our children, particularly "Very Like a Whale" for older children learning about similes and metaphors, and "Lines Fraught With Naught But Thought" for teens learning philosophy. Hilaire Belloc's amusing *A Bad Child's Book of Beasts* is another wonderful resource. Edgar Guest may quickly become a favorite in our home once we read his humorous, sentimental poems celebrating family life, including "Tied Down," "The Old-Time Family," "Morning Brigands," "Baby's Got a Tooth," and "Being Brave at Night." Nor must we forget the legacy of Catholic poets, from Joyce Kilmer's "Citizen of the World," "Prayer of a Soldier in France," and "St. Laurence" to Phyllis Whitney's humorous verses about various saints, including "The Giveaway," "Simeon Styles," "Paterfamilias," and "Once There Were Three Irishmen." Robert Hugh Benson's *An Alphabet of Saints* consists of twenty-six clever poems about saints that our children may enjoy reading or memorizing. Nor should we neglect the classics, such as "Tiger, Tiger" by William Blake, "The Arrow and the Song" by Longfellow, "The Daffodils" by Wordsworth, or "The Highwayman" by Alfred Noyes.

Sometimes poems can enhance our history lessons, such as "Columbus" by Joaquin Miller or Stephen Vincent Benet's collection of humorous portraits in verse, *Book of Americans*. We can encourage our children to write different types of poetry, too, including limericks, which are always fun. If we can find a collection of limericks such as *Laughable Limericks* edited by Sara and John E. Brewton, we should grab it—and read them a loud together some rainy day or when everyone's down with the flu. Perhaps they could write poems for each other on St. Valentine's Day or on birthdays. We can write down potential topics for poems on small pieces of paper and have each child pick one and write a poem about the topic he picks, like "washing dishes," "riding a bike," "my favorite saint," or "penguins." Upper grade school children or teens should try writing a sonnet at least once in their school years, after studying some of the well-known sonnets by Shakespeare, Elizabeth Barrett Browning, and Keats, as well as the less familiar sonnet "The Rosary" by Joyce Kilmer. We can also have poetry recitations once or twice a month where every child chooses a poem to memorize and recite. This strengthens the memory in a fun way, and also gives the child a deeper intimacy and appreciation for the poem he is learning. Poetry nights can be made especially fun if we end the occasion with a special dessert or family game.

Children should also sometimes read plays. A. A. Milne has some very amusing plays for grade school children, while older children will find the plays of George Bernard Shaw highly readable. (Shaw was a socialist, and our children may enjoy finding traces of his political leanings in his plays. His best plays for youngsters are probably *Pygmalion* and *Arms and the Man*.) Oscar Wilde's plays are very readable, also, especially his comical *The Importance of Being Earnest*. Of course, every teen should read several plays by Shakespeare; we can choose a version with footnotes to explain the obsolete words. Ignatius Press offers "Critical Editions" of some of Shakespeare's plays, as well as an entire book, *Through Shakespeare's Eyes* by Joseph Pearce, which reveals the Catholic dimension of three of Shakespeare's works. These are highly recommended for a true grasp of Shakespeare's plays.

Our children may enjoy putting on a few scenes from a play they've read, or they may want to write and perform their own short plays. Trying to find an inexpensive, family-friendly play to attend can be harder than finding a free concert, but we can check out the productions of local colleges or high schools in our area. We may be pleasantly surprised.

Dancing is one more way of expressing culture. We must be careful that the way our children dance is not immodest or unseemly, which is the kind of dancing that today's music encourages. Rather, we can teach our children to swing dance, polka, waltz, or fox trot. If we don't know these dances ourselves, we can look in the library for a video explaining how. (We may want to watch the video ourselves in the evenings when the children are in bed, and then, the next day, teach our children what we have learned.) Of course, we'll also have to find some music with the appropriate tempo to dance to. Square dancing and folk dancing are also a lot of fun, although square dancing requires a larger group of people and may therefore be harder to arrange. Dancing not only imparts culture, it grants us a new outlet to express emotion and beauty; develops a certain discipline, grace, concentration, and coordination; and, best of all, provides indoor exercise during the winter months

There are so many beautiful expressions of culture with which we can fill our home. Let us not be satisfied with unwholesome, poor quality, or even immoral substitutes. Rather, like St. Paul, "whatsoever things are true, whatsoever modest, whatsoever just, whatsoever holy, whatsoever lovely, whatsoever of good fame, if there be any virtue, if any praise of discipline: think on these things" (Philippians 4:8). True culture lifts up our hearts and minds to the wonder and goodness of God, Who not only creates beauty, but creates a creature who can also create beauty.

# 19

## ART APPRECIATION

*"Because commending a work of art
is always a tribute to the artist, beauty is
always a song about God, and those
who thrill in the artifact are singing to him."*

—FR. THOMAS DUBAY

ART is, of course, another important outlet for cultural expression. Children love looking at pictures, so art appreciation is particularly pleasant to share with them. The main obstacle to art appreciation is finding suitable art prints. There is no need to spend a fortune on expensive art books, although a really good one may provide a solid foundation for our art library. There are many options here. Used book sales sometimes have art books for sale.

We may be reluctant to share with our children art books that feature paintings of nudes. Even children who seem mature for their age and who do not engage in crude comments may find unclad figures a temptation at a time of budding sexual awareness, which they have not yet learned to control. Sensitive to our children's needs, we can efface troublesome images with black magic marker, or, if the paper is glossy and resists marker, use white-out or simply cut the problematic pages out. We may find that many art books have too many nudes to obliterate them all; then we can consider cutting out the good paintings and compiling them into one or more scrapbooks. We can organize the paintings by artist, or by the country the artists are from, or by topic: for example, landscapes in one scrapbook, portraits in another, and historical paintings in another. One scrapbook could compile the life of Christ in art, and another paintings of saints. Or we could fill one scrapbook with Christmas art, which we can look over as a family during the Christmas season. Christmas cards that feature paintings by the old masters can be used for this, as well. Other sources for artwork can be found online; we can find nice reproductions of famous paintings on the Internet and print them on a color printer, to fill some gaps in our scrapbooks. (This can be done at the library for a small fee if we don't own a color printer.) Pencil drawings or woodcuts by famous artists could be printed out in black-and-white at a lower price.

Dover Publications also offers inexpensive books of color postcards by Leonardo da Vinci, Gainsborough, Renoir, and many other painters, as well as inexpensive books featuring drawings by famous artists, and even coloring books of famous paintings. (See doverpublications.com or check out Emmanuel Books.) Dover's stickers of famous paintings can also be used to make cards for "Memory" or "Go Fish" or "Old Maid"—but this requires ordering two copies of each set, as Dover sticker sets contain no duplicates. This is a very hands-on method to familiarize our children with great works of art. Catholic Heritage Curricula (chcweb.com) sells some art appreciation programs that provide not only art prints, but also lessons on how to appreciate each work of art.

Another wonderful resource is Ernest Raboff's series of art books for children. Each of his books focuses on a single artist and features color reproductions of the artist's work, along with very simple commentaries on each piece. While these books seem to target primary school children, children of any age may enjoy them and learn something new. Elizabeth Ripley's biographies of various artists are also very educational, featuring black and white reproductions; her books are a little longer than Raboff's and are aimed at grade school children, but again, they would be informative and interesting for children of any age. However, with both Raboff's and Ripley's books, occasionally there will be a painting of a nude, and we must decide how we are going to deal with that. If we take the books out of the library, we obviously can't cut out or ink out the objectionable pictures; however, we could tell our children to skip certain pages, or put the books out of reach except when we actually are reading them with our children, depending on their maturity. We could also use paper clips to attach two pages together so the children won't look at the forbidden pages by mistake.

When looking for artwork, we should try to find art that will appeal to all of our children, as well as some art that may not appeal to them, but will broaden their ideas about art. For example, boys will like "The Lion Hunt" by Delacroix, "Daniel in the Lions' Den" by Rubens, "The Officer of the Guard" by Gerricault, "The Gulf Stream" by Winslow Homer, or any of the exciting Western scenes by Remington. Girls may be more attracted to portraits of pretty ladies by Sir George Romney or Thomas Gainsborough, breathtaking landscapes by Claude Lorrain or Albert Bierstadt, and the cute babies by Mary Cassatt. The bright colors of Renoir's Impressionist paintings will probably attract them all, as will the truly beautiful religious art of Raphael, Caravaggio, Murillo, and Velasquez. The somber, mysterious moods of Rembrandt and the pale, elongated figures of El Greco may take more time to grow on some children, although most children will appreciate at least one characteristic of El Greco's artwork—how easy it is to recognize! Early Renaissance art, such as work done by Fra Angelico, Giotto, or Jan Van Eyke, may appear stiff and stilted to our children before they realize that techniques of achieving three dimensional perspective, facial expressions, and bodily gestures were just being developed by these and other artists for the first time. We want our children to appreciate art, so we can to choose artwork that will please them most of the time, and only occasionally select artwork that will stretch their tastes.

We should try to talk about different works of art. We can ask the children if they like the artwork, and why or why not, how the painting makes them feel (or how they think the painter wanted it to make them feel). We can talk about the symbolism in the paintings, especially religious paintings like Botticelli's. We can talk about how the artist used lighting and other techniques to capture a certain effect. We can discuss whether the person in the painting is young or old, rich or poor, and whether the painting is detailed or slapdash, and how that influences the overall effect. We can introduce our children to Impressionism, and if we have a really good print, we can show the children how the fuzzy colors that we see when we look closely suddenly appear quite realistic when seen from a distance. We can talk about how different historical periods and philosophies are reflected in art. Renaissance art shows the religious fervor of the period; the Romantic movement of the nineteenth century led to a proliferation of paintings of nature and children, both of which the Romantics idealized; Impressionism, which tried to catch fleeting impressions rather than objective, photographic details, may be a product of philosophical relativism, which declares there is no objective reality, and that truth is different for each person; and modern art, which portrays no objective reality at all, is the fruit of nihilism, a belief in nothing. We can look up the lives of some of the artists; Fra Angelico has been declared blessed by the Church, while Peter Paul Rubens was a daily communicant. Other artists lived less admirable lives, but we can often understand their work better by knowing something about the context in which they painted.

All of these issues, and more, can be discussed over a long period of time as we sit and look at art books together—or we can display one piece of artwork at lunch, to be discussed while eating. Our children can try to copy great works of art on their own.

If we live near an art museum, we can take our children to see some great art in person. (We may want to take photos of our family's favorite works so our trip to the museum will be remembered and appreciated for a longer time; however, cameras with a flash are not usually permitted in art museums, so we will need to either own or borrow a camera whose flash can be turned off.) Very tactile children may have trouble not touching exhibits, so we can adjust the length of our visit to our children's needs. Many art museums offer free admission on Sundays.

Our goal is to familiarize our children with the great works of art and to help them to develop a love and appreciation of art that expresses the best in man—that which is good, true, and noble. While we are engaged in this enjoyable endeavor, we may be surprised at what else our children will learn—about religion, about philosophy, about history, about life, about expressing themselves, and about creating their own works of art. Let us not get so bogged down with the basic core curriculum that we miss introducing our children to the beautiful heritage of art that has inspired Western civilization for centuries.

# 20

## PHYSICAL ACTIVITY

*"The body also stands in need of exercise,
and in all stations men owe several exterior
duties both to others and themselves, and to
neglect any of these, upon pretence of giving the
preference to prayer, would be a false
devotion and dangerous illusion."*

—FR. ALBAN BUTLER

FEW homeschooling mothers put aside a day every week to teach gym to their children. Instead, most just make sure that their children get plenty of exercise. However, this is easier said than done, especially in the winter when it is too cold or too wet to go out. If we can't let the children go out to play, we can try to find ways of exercising inside without tearing the house apart. We should teach our children how to stretch before strenuous exercise, and how to do basic exercises, such as jumping jacks, sit-ups, push-ups, and running in place; however, while it is good for our children to be familiar with these exercises, they will not want, or need, to do them most of the time. Instead, we can try teaching them to dance, especially the polka, and get a few CDs with polka music. We can get a punching bag for boys (or girls) who need an outlet of a more aggressive nature. We can try a trampoline for the children to jump on. A ping-pong table in the basement or the garage, if we have space, can also sharpen our children's coordination while providing some exercise, too. (Actually, if we have a large dining room table, we can buy a net that attaches to any table and play ping-pong that way.) A nerf basketball game can also help release some energy indoors. If the cold weather is not too severe, we can occasionally bundle everyone up and go out for a very brisk walk (although if we have babies or toddlers, this may not be the best option).

During the warmer months, of course, getting our children to exercise is easier. Jumping rope, bicycling, taking walks, throwing a Frisbee or a baseball, or organizing a game of tennis or kickball, are excellent outlets for our children's energy. Unstructured, spontaneous play outdoors is best of all.

Perhaps even more important than finding ways for our children to exercise is finding ways that we can exercise, too. Most children will find a release for their energy, even if it's running up and down the stairs until they drive their mothers crazy, but all too often, we mothers do not take care of our own need for physical exertion. We feel exhausted from picking up clutter and scrubbing the floors and running up to the attic for yet another book, without realizing that none of these activities provides the physical outlet that our bodies need. We must rack our brains to find some way to fit in a little exercise for ourselves; perhaps we could take a walk or a jog or a bike ride in the mornings, before our children get up, or after dinner when our husband is home, or take a walk with the children during the day in fair weather. Or we could pick up a second-hand stationary bike that we can use for half an hour while the little ones are napping. At the very least we could join our children in their polka dancing.

Sometimes it can be very difficult to get the physical exercise we need, considering our busy schedule and numerous responsibilities. Yet we really need to make some effort to find some kind of pleasant exercise for our own good and for our children's. While we shouldn't become obsessed with our appearance or with reaching a certain magic weight or size in clothes, which would hardly be the kind of example that we want to model to our girls, moderate, regular exercise will keep us trim enough that our girls don't think of stay-at-home, homeschooling mothers as unattractive drudges. Even more importantly, physical exercise will clear our minds, lighten our moods, and provide us with more energy to accomplish our daily tasks. We will be not only healthier but happier and more stable emotionally and spiritually, better equipped to tend to the needs of our youngsters. We humans are a body-soul composite, and body and mind have tremendous influence on one another. A healthy, disciplined body cannot help but contribute to a healthier, more wholesome mind and soul.

Moreover, as with anything else, our example will teach our children to continue to take good care of their bodies as they grow and mature. Running and jumping are not just for little ones—they're for all of God's children who delight in, and take care of, the beautiful bodies He has given us.

# 21

## PRAYER

*"Prayer is a place of refuge for every
worry, a foundation for cheerfulness,
a source of constant happiness,
a protection against sadness."*

—ST. JOHN CHRYSOSTOM

MOTHERS live lives of constant self-giving. Our time is not our own. Even our meals are not our own, for what mother does not find herself rising many times from the table to cut up some food or to bring in the dessert? Even our sleep is interrupted at times, especially if there is a baby in the house or if the children are sick. Furthermore, any "free" time we do find usually goes to housework or lesson plans or running errands to pick up something for our children—it's not really about our own needs at all.

Fortunately, as mothers, we feel happy and fulfilled when our time and energy are spent on those we love. Nevertheless, we do need to make sure we put aside some time every day for our own needs. As we have mentioned, we need some form of exercise, which refreshes both mind and body, lifting our spirits and keeping our bodies healthy. We also need some way to socialize or converse with other adults, particularly our husbands, but also on occasion some other mothers like ourselves who can sympathize with our doubts and worries and share our joy over our successes. However, even more important than our need for exercise and adult conversation is our need for prayer. We absolutely must make time every day to build our relationship with Our Lord. If we aren't growing spiritually, then we are regressing. There is no standing still in the spiritual life.

Praying with our children is a wonderful and necessary custom, but since we often find ourselves focused on making sure they are behaving properly—kneeling up straight and not mumbling, for example—we should find a time when we can be alone with Christ. If necessary, we can sometimes combine this time with our exercise; we can pray while we walk or jog. We could use a walkman or an iPod with an audio recording of the rosary, or listen to the Gospel or some other holy book. Spiritual reading should be included in our daily regime if at all possible. A good spiritual book challenges our spiritual *status quo* and encourages us to grow in holiness and wisdom, as well as inspiring us to pause and pray as we read.

We may be tempted to let our spiritual reading slide because we are constantly confronted by so many immediate chores that need doing. We may even feel slightly guilty for spending time on ourselves. However, we must remember that our own job goes beyond fixing meals, doing laundry, and correcting papers; we are the molders of our children's souls. Our mood sets the atmosphere of the household; our perspective shapes the opinions and ideas of our children, and our spiritual state can either limit or expand their spiritual horizons. We want to raise our children to be saints, but we cannot give them what we do not have; therefore, we must become as saintly as we can, and we cannot become saintly without daily converse with the Source of all sanctity.

In addition to this quiet time spent with Christ alone, we can lift our hearts to God frequently during the various activities of the day. Some people say that we should not waste prayers on trivial events; but this was not the attitude of the saints, who wanted every aspect of their lives tinged with the spiritual. Nothing is too small or too silly to speak to Our Lord about; after all, He knows how many hairs we have on our heads. St. Gertrude the Great was not ashamed to ask Our Lord to help her find a needle she dropped in some straw, so why can't we ask St. Anthony to help us find a puzzle piece, or St. Lawrence to help us get dinner done on time, or the Divine Child to help our own children learn the multiplication table, just as He helped St. Rose of Lima learn how to read? While engaged in the awkward task of helping a child learn how to ride a bicycle, we can lift our hearts to the child's guardian angel or patron saint for assistance. How else can we, as mothers, follow St. Paul's injunction to "pray without ceasing" (1 Thessalonians 5:17)?

Christianity goes beyond merely fulfilling our duties and avoiding sin as best we can. Such a dry, barebones Christianity will hardly inspire or attract our children to virtue or holiness. No, we must immerse ourselves in the faith, hope, and love of our religion, and our joy will bubble over and communicate itself irresistibly to all we meet. During our time set aside for spiritual reading and prayer, we must reflect often on the goodness and love of God and all of His perfections; on the brevity of this life and the eternity of the hereafter; and on the many other glorious truths of our faith. During the day, we must habituate ourselves to speaking to Our Lord about all the little events and worries of each hour so we can eventually view everything from a spiritual perspective. This way, we will steep ourselves in godly prayers and reflections so that we may come to love God with our whole being and long to be with Him more than anything else in this world; until, like St. Paul, we can say, "And I live, now not I; but Christ liveth in me" (Galatians 2:20). Then our faith, hope, and love will indeed be contagious and will spread from us to our children, inspiring them to deepen their own relationship with Christ.

# 22

## HUMOR

*"God deliver me from sullen saints!"*

—ST. TERESA OF AVILA

HUMILITY and patience take years to learn and master, but a sense of humor can go far in helping us to learn both. If we can laugh at ourselves, then we are well on our way. If we can learn to laugh at aggravations and disappointments, then our vale of tears will be sweetened and our souls will grow closer to God.

It is not always easy to laugh when things go wrong—when the baby gets into his older brother's magic markers or a child throws up over brand new school books. Sometimes we feel more like indulging in a temper tantrum. But anger, whether expressed in shouts or grumbles, will not help the situation; anger makes any situation worse. When we encounter a situation that displeases us, let us immediately raise our hearts to God. We can say, "I offer this to You, Lord," or, even better, "I know this comes from Your most loving Heart, Lord, and I accept it and offer it to You with all the love in my heart." Then we can return our gaze to the situation at hand and face it with peace and joy. If our children are upset or hurt, we can try to ease their distress—and our own—by making a joke. Sometimes all we just need to think about how we will feel about this incident ten years from now. Right now, the situation is nothing less than a disaster; in ten or twenty years, it will be a humorous and unforgettable memory. Let's take the long-term view of each incident.

Gloomy faces and sharp tongues do not reflect holiness of soul. Rather, holiness finds expression in a joyful acceptance of God's inscrutable Will, along with the understanding that all of this is passing, and that as difficult as life can seem at times, we know that our side wins in the end. Our joy will frequently be expressed in humor, and humor, in turn, can help us not to lose our inner joy, even in the most trying moments.

Not only will humor help us to grow in holiness, but it will help our children, as well. If they see us getting upset or annoyed over every little thing that changes our plans on a day-to-day basis, then they will most likely learn to react the same way. However, if they see us react with peace and humor to the petty aggravations in life, then they will learn to react that way, too. Every moment that we are with our children is a teaching moment. We may not be sitting at the table with schoolbooks open, but they are still learning from everything they see us say and do. Let us be conscious of the tremendous power we have over their impressionable minds!

This long-term view can help us through times of sickness, too. No mother likes to see telltale symptoms of a cold or flu that is about to descend upon the entire family for the next week or two. The more children in the house, the longer the illness will take to pass through the entire family. Some years our family will seem to catch every virus that goes through the neighborhood. Not only does sickness entail lots of extra work, worry, and sometimes sleepless nights on our part, but sickness often means cancellation of all plans to go out of the house or to have people over, lest we infect another family. If we catch the sickness, too, then we have the burden of trying to rest and get well while doing the exhausting job of tending sick children. Overall, sickness is a time of self-sacrifice, a thwarting of our plans and our will, a carrying of the cross. Yet these days of tending sick children are days to be treasured just like any others, for these are the days when we show our love in action, by the gentle and sympathetic nursing of each child. These, too, are memories that will long be remembered, both by the parents (with laughs and shudders) and by the children, who will always fondly appreciate the tenderness shown by their parents when they were feeling "icky." Let us foresee now the laughter and affection we will feel later for these challenging days, and strive to find things to laugh about so our memories will be even sweeter. Maybe we can put aside a joke book or some other humorous book to read aloud to our children when the family is sick. We could also set aside a special CD with soothing songs or a particularly funny old radio program to create a comforting atmosphere in times of sickness. St. Philip Neri, who used to read joke books in public out of humility so that people wouldn't think he was a saint, can help us find an appropriate book or CD to help us through these difficult days.

True, we mothers are imperfect, and we may not always be the patient nurses we would like to be, especially when we suspect a child is exaggerating his symptoms to receive more attention, or when we are drained from caring for sick children for days on end while fighting off similar symptoms ourselves. Still, let us take a few moments during these hectic times to reflect on how the sickness draws our family together. No one can leave the house; our children lie in their beds or on the sofa, commiserating with each other, the healthier ones getting a cup of water for the sicker ones or trying to entertain them. Sometimes children who never get along when they are healthy suddenly become inseparable when one or both is sick. As we cradle the feverish ones, wipe the noses of the sniffling ones, clean up after the vomiting ones, and read softly to them all as they snuggle close to us, we know we are showing our children what love means. This is our school of love in action.

# 23

## THE GREATEST LESSON

*"Do you realize that Jesus is there in the
tabernacle for you, for you alone? He burns
with the desire to come into your heart."*

—ST. THERESE OF LISIEUX

THE greatest, most important lesson that we can teach
our children cannot be found in any syllabus or curricula. The greatest lesson is to bring them regularly to
make a visit to the Blessed Sacrament.

A visit to the Blessed Sacrament will teach them better
than a dozen lectures on transubstantiation that Christ is
present, Body and Blood, Soul and Divinity, in the Holy
Eucharist. Otherwise, why go to church when there's no
Mass going on? We go only because Someone is there
to visit. And if we make visiting the Blessed Sacrament a
priority, a regular part of our family's schedule, then our
children will learn that the Holy Eucharist is central to
their spiritual life—"the source and summit" of Christian
life, as Pope John Paul II so aptly said.

By visiting the Blessed Sacrament, our children will have the opportunity to develop a more personal relationship with Christ. In the silence of a dimly lit church, our children will have the time to pray, to adore, to reflect, and to simply sit in God's presence and listen to His voice in their hearts. They can encounter Christ in a more meaningful, more intimate way than ever before.

If possible, we should supply age-appropriate prayerbooks for visits to the Blessed Sacrament: the Divine Praises, an English translation of St. Thomas Aquinas' "Adoro te devote," acts of consecration and reparation to the Sacred Heart, or a selection of litanies will show children that prayer is not always about asking for things. These prayers can also introduce children to meditative prayer, as can the rosary and the Stations of the Cross. If we can't find, or can't afford, prayerbooks with these prayers, we could find these prayers on the Internet, print them out, and decorate them with religious stickers. Older children might want to bring some spiritual reading. The pamphlet *I Wait for You* by Sr. Josefa Menendez or *Visits to the Blessed Sacrament* by St. Alphonsus Liguori (both published by TAN) may help older children develop a devotion to the Holy Eucharist. All of these tools can be invaluable in teaching our children how to pray or in helping them combat distractions or boredom during a visit. Nevertheless, the children should also be encouraged to spend some time praying in their own words to develop a greater sense of intimacy and closeness to Christ.

How long to make the visit will depend on the ages and temperaments of our children. High schoolers might be able to manage an hour, while most grade school children could do twenty or thirty minutes. Preschoolers, kindergarteners, and very active primary school children could stay anywhere from five to fifteen minutes; we'll be able to tell easily enough when our little ones become restless. Of course, if our children's ages span many years, problems arise. We could bring only a few children at a time, or we could bring them all but take the younger children outside for the last ten or twenty minutes while the older ones continue to pray. (If the church is attached to a school, there may be a playground to use.) If there is no one else in the church, we could take the younger children around to look at and identify the scenes portrayed in the stained glass windows and statues, while the older ones pray. If time permits, we can make the trip a little more memorable by stopping at the library or a craft store or even an ice cream parlor on the way home.

Sometimes we may have trouble finding a church that is unlocked during the week. We can inquire if there is an adoration chapel in our diocese, or even ask our parish priest when the church is left open. Another option would be to make a visit when the priest is hearing confessions, usually late Saturday afternoons. If we want to go during the week, we might ask the receptionist at the rectory to unlock the church for us if we come during office hours. Hopefully, we will be able to find an open church that is not too far away.

One of the best benefits of bringing our children to visit the Blessed Sacrament is that we, too, have a chance to pray, adore, and listen to Our Lord—in short, to spend time with the One Who loves us most. A homeschooling mother's life is often so busy and hectic that her prayer life suffers. Family rosaries may be spent admonishing inattentive children; private spiritual reading is all too often interrupted by urgent pleas. Half an hour in a silent church once or twice a week can rejuvenate and refresh us for our demanding life at home. Even a few moments in His presence comfort our soul, assure us of His love, remind us of what is truly important, and prepare us for the challenges lying ahead. Most of all, these moments allow us an opportunity to grow closer to Our Lord—our Beginning and our End, our Life, our Love, our Strength.

# 24

## HOMESCHOOLING DURING PREGNANCY

*"'Do you want a boy or a girl?' Do not, under*
*any circumstances, answer this question.*
*If you say you want a girl and have*
*a boy, somebody is bound to tell him*
*over and over through the years:*
*'Now I know why your mother wanted a girl.'*
*The same goes for vice versa. If you feel you*
*must answer this question, I recommend*
*either of two answers: (a) 'Not particularly' or*
*(b) 'Of course,' depending on how nauseous*
*you have been that day."*

—TERESA BLOOMINGDALE, COLUMNIST,
AUTHOR, AND MOTHER OF 10

HOMESCHOOLING during pregnancy presents unique, but not insurmountable challenges. When we are experiencing typical pregnancy symptoms, such as nausea, vomiting, exhaustion, and so forth, and we're struggling to manage the most basic household chores and

the simplest meals, sitting down to teach long division—
or even worse, algebra—may seem far beyond our current
capabilities. But this is not the time to start enrolling our
children in the nearest school. Pregnancy will pass, and in
the meantime, there are ways to keep homeschooling and
still avoid insanity.

The key is to keep our priorities straight. Our own
physical, emotional, and spiritual well-being must come
before lessons. We can't be effective teachers—or even
mothers—if we neglect our own needs. Our children will
suffer more from having an ill or emotionally unstable
mother than from skipping lessons for a few weeks while
we get some extra rest. We can take a few days off when we
need to. Maybe we can't take off the whole nine months,
but a few days or even weeks won't hurt. When we do
choose to do lessons, we can take it easy. We can lie on
the sofa while a young one reads aloud to us or answers
catechism questions. We can encourage our children to
work independently by writing a schedule so they know
what they are expected to accomplish each day. This is not
the time to plan science experiments or other complicated
projects. We can do a whole month of science projects
when we feel better if we so desire. (Often expectant mothers have more energy during the second trimester—but, if
not, we can wait until after the baby is born, or until the
weekend when dad can play scientist with them.) For now,
we can find activities that don't require much help from
us. We can even have the children help each other, drill-
ing each other on math facts, state capitals, or catechism.

An older child could help a younger child with some math problems, and a younger child could help an older child with straight memorization.

Here is the time to rely a little more on the learning environment we have sought to create in our household. We can find some particularly appealing books from the library or the attic and leave them around, or allow the children to choose which ones to read for lessons. We can trust our children's natural curiosity and creativity to take over. Given the right kind of environment, they won't stop learning just because we've stopped assigning work. They may not learn exactly what we would choose them to learn, but they will learn just as much, if not more, because of their freedom to choose and their interest in the subject. Further, if we are too tired or too sick to get up every time the children encounter an obstacle, they'll learn some problem-solving skills, as well. Who knows? They may even learn to work together and help each other.

All of this might sound a bit utopian. "Your children might keep learning, but mine won't," we may think. Well, our children may not look like they're learning; they may not be filling out worksheets and taking notes on what they read; but if they're reading good books, they're learning. If they're creating—writing, drawing, painting, or building—they're learning. If they're playing almost anything but a game of pure luck, they're learning. (Even a game of luck could teach them the principles of probability, but that's stretching it a little.) Children are learning constantly, as long as they're awake. Enjoy observing how they use this extra time. We might be surprised at what they come up with.

It's tempting, during pregnancy, to feel guilty that we're not spending enough time with our children. Laundry and meals are about all we can manage, yet we also want to read to our children, teach them, play games with them, drive them to a dozen outside activities, and more. Let's not be unrealistic. Pregnancy is passing. Our children won't have a deprived childhood because we didn't read to them much or take them out very often for a few months. Our children can see what we're doing and how we're feeling. They can see that we've set aside our normal activities, not so we can go out by ourselves and have fun, but because we're temporarily incapacitated. Even the youngest child can sense that. Although we're not busy doing projects with them, we haven't left them. We're right here on the sofa (or in the bathroom), ready to kiss a bruised knee or listen to a tale of woe. We are with them, for good or for ill, every day and night. Our physical presence means more than anything; it speaks volumes about what—or who—is most precious to us.

Eventually, as the children grow, they will learn another valuable lesson from watching our pregnancies. They will remember our illness, our tiredness, our struggle to do housework, and our sacrifice of the enjoyable activities we gave up, and they'll remember *why* we made these sacrifices: to bring forth new life. Thus, they will learn one of life's most valuable lessons: people are more important than things, and new life is a gift to treasure, to suffer for, and to cherish over comfort and worldly goods.

At first we may wonder if it's fair to our children to continue homeschooling during pregnancy, when we know our energy and ability to teach will be so greatly diminished. Yet by witnessing our pregnancy, day in and day out, our children will learn lessons they could never learn in a classroom—lessons about independence, problem-solving, self-sacrifice, and love.

# 25

# HOMESCHOOLING WITH
# A NEWBORN

*"But from what benighted dens can these*
*people have crawled, that they did not know*
*that women were brave?... Where did they*
*come from? Or, what is a still more apposite*
*question, where do they think they come from?*
*Do they think they fell from the moon,*
*or were really found under cabbage-leaves, or*
*brought over the sea by storks?... Should we any*
*of us be here at all if women were not brave?*
*Are we not all trophies of that war and*
*triumph? Does not every man stand on the*
*earth like a graven statue as the monument*
*of the valor of a woman?"*

—G. K. CHESTERTON

THE discomforts of pregnancy and anxiety about childbirth can make a mother's life much more difficult, never mind homeschooling. Although Scriptures speak about the pains of childbearing quite frequently, even comparing the apostles' sorrow over Christ's death to them (cf. John 16:21), there is little mention of a mother's physical trials in works by Catholic writers. The above quote is one of the rare exceptions. A pregnant or *postpartum* mother might do well to hang this quote where she can see it often to remind herself what a wondrous thing she is accomplishing and how truly heroic her vocation is. With this in mind, she must not expect too much of herself in the weeks immediately after giving birth.

There are, of course, advantages in homeschooling, even with a new baby. After giving birth, we can thank the Lord that, as homeschoolers, our children will be able to spend the precious first days with their new brother or sister instead of being whisked away to school for most of their waking hours. We can be glad that our children can see firsthand the time and attention we lavish on our newborn as a testimony to the sacredness of every human life, however tiny. We can rejoice that our children are granted the opportunity to help out around the house during this exciting but exhausting time, especially with toddlers who would be too young to go to school and whom we'd have to manage by ourselves along with the newborn, if we weren't homeschooling the older children.

However, we must acknowledge that continuing to homeschool after a baby is born can be as challenging as homeschooling during pregnancy. Fortunately, the flexibility of homeschooling can enable us to manage, even if our home looks even less like a classroom than ever before. If we have trained our children to work independently during pregnancy, then they may be able to continue lessons without missing a single day. We may need to prepare a little before the baby comes to make this possible— we can make up a schedule for each day of the week, print out or photocopy any relevant crossword puzzles or other sheets they'll need, and be sure they have the books on the subjects they'll be studying. Of course, teaching new concepts may have to go on the back burner for a few weeks, but the children can read history or practice arithmetic without us. Younger children who can't do much independent work may end up with a few weeks' break, but this will hardly do any harm. Our first concern must be our own health and the health of the baby. A new mother who doesn't rest whenever she can may find her milk supply depleting, or may wind up with mastitis, a painful breast infection that requires lots of rest to cure. We must nap whenever we can until the baby sleeps through the night. If this means skipping lessons occasionally, this is a small price to pay for our mental and physical health. If we can't spend the time we'd like on housework or lessons, we must remember we'd have even less time for these things if we became ill.

However, once the baby's feedings are established, we can resume some lessons while breastfeeding, as long as we are not too tired. A young child can read to us while we nurse, and we can read to them while nursing (at least until the baby gets old enough to start grabbing the book). Some ambitious mothers move around while nursing and can do math or play a board game during feedings.

Others may prefer to sit in an armchair with their feet up until the feeding is over. If we are bottlefeeding, we may not be able to hold a book as easily during feedings, but we could still listen to a child read or recite; our children could even hold the book up for us if they are really determined to have mom read to them! Nursing the baby is also a good time to say the family rosary together. Whatever style of feeding our baby we choose, lessons don't have to come to a complete halt just because we're nursing a baby eight to ten times a day. Of course, daily feedings can also offer the opportunity for heart-to-heart talks with our children.

Delegation is even more crucial during *postpartum* days than any other time. Children can learn to take care of younger siblings' needs, prepare simple meals, wash dishes, do laundry, and perform other safe household tasks. These chores may not be part of a typical classroom education, but they are useful life skills that our children will need as they grow older. "Home economics" is usually reserved for teenaged girls, but boys and girls of almost any age will benefit from participating in housework. Furthermore, the development of new skills and the knowledge that they are contributing significantly to the family's well-being will build self-esteem and confidence.

Most of all during those blissful but crazy *postpartum* days, we learn to reject the materialist principle that places things above people: we have to give up perfectionism in all material things and focus on the people around us. From dirty floors to unfinished lessons, none of our usual preoccupations is as important as our children. Cooking, cleaning, and teaching must take a back seat to loving—loving our new baby and sharing that love with everyone else in the family. This time is too precious to spoil by worrying about home-cooked meals and missed days of school. Whether we know it or not, our children will be learning and absorbing just as much in these days as ever—primarily that bringing a new baby into the home is a happy, if sometimes challenging, experience, one that demands cooperation and teamwork and brings a special love and joy. They'll learn the satisfaction of helping others, the thrill of tiny fingers clasping their own, and the wonder of welcoming a new life into this world.

# 26

## SPENDING TIME WITH
## OUR CHILDREN

*"All the wealth in the world cannot
be compared with the happiness of
living together happily united."*
—BLESSED MARGARET D'YOUVILLE

ONE of the very best aspects of homeschooling is that
we are able to spend huge quantities of time with
our children. How often we hear from older parents that
their children's childhood went by too quickly! While these
precious years go by quickly for homeschoolers as well, at
least we know that we are spending the maximum amount
of time with our children; we will not look back with regret
at all the time we wasted away from them.

Or will we? Even homeschoolers can get caught up in
the materialistic culture we live in. We may find ourselves
spending too much time surfing the Internet, running
errands, or chauffeuring children from one scheduled
activity to another instead of truly being present to our
children.

As mentioned before, the mistake of materialism is to place things above people. We are too busy with things—schoolwork, housework, the Internet, or some other material object—to truly cherish each child. When a child breaks something, do we first comfort the child or grumble over the damage done? When a child spills milk, do we speak impatiently as we rush to clean up the spill? Do we brush off a child's questions because we are busy? Does most of our speech to our children fit into the categories of nagging or correcting? Do we listen when our child speaks to us? When we spend time with our children, are we always distracted by the phone or the television, or do we truly look in our child's eyes, asking him his opinion and listening attentively to his answer? Do we find time to spend with each child one-on-one, either in the house, baking together, playing a board game together, playing outside, taking a walk, or running errands together?

If we allow the materialistic mindset to engulf us, we may even decide to limit the number of children we have without grave reason. What else can we call it when we value a large house, annual vacations, expensive curricula, field trips, or new cars over the incomparable gift of a new human life? What else can we call it when we are not willing to sacrifice our own pleasure to endure the discomforts and inconveniences of pregnancy in order to bring a new baby into the world? This is the very height of materialism, when we consider any material good or worldly advantage preferable to an immortal soul created by God.

Yes, we have to do housework. Yes, we need some time to pursue our own interests or to talk on the phone to other adults. We must teach our children not to interrupt us at certain times. Nevertheless, we must remember that we will always have more housework to do. Even if we ever finished the gargantuan task of washing and folding all the dirty clothes, we could wash the curtains or dust or do something else. Housework we will always have with us. If we really value our children above our things, then we will make spending time with them a top priority. Moreover, we will become less annoyed at the havoc they wreak around the house. We will look at a torn book and be glad our children enjoyed reading it so many times. We will see broken toys and be grateful that our children are healthy and lively. We will see clutter on the floor and the table and smile because our children have the space and freedom to explore, create, and play. Yes, we must teach our children to take care of their possessions. Yes, we must teach them to clean up after themselves. But we must not lose sight of the fact that toys and books are merely tools to help us reach a higher goal, whereas our children are people, infinitely more important than any material object, destined by God to praise Him forever in heaven. It is our fearsome task to mold these vulnerable souls to be pleasing to their heavenly Father.

We homeschooling mothers are incredibly busy with innumerable responsibilities. But let us not forget our primary, most important, responsibility of nurturing and loving our children. Let us play with our children, talk to them, and cherish time spent with each one. Let us put aside time whenever we can to do something fun with them. If we really need to do housework, let us try to involve our children in the work or to chat with them while we work. Often we can find something little for a child to do in the kitchen while we're making dinner or in the laundry room while we're switching laundry. We could also play word games while we work. For example, the game "geography" is a game where one person names a geographical place and the next person has to name another place that begins with the last letter of the place the first person named; for example, one might say, "New York," and the next person might say, "Kentucky," and then "Yugoslavia," and so on. Another game that we can play while doing housework might be a rhyming game where we think up clues to help the person guess the word; for example, "It rhymes with 'habit' and it's a small animal that likes carrots." The level of difficulty of this game can be adjusted to the age of the participants. We could also play "Twenty Questions." Best of all, we could just spend time chatting about what they're reading, what they're thinking about, what's bothering them, or what they're looking forward to.

All too soon the little hands we hold will grow big, and we will find ourselves looking up, instead of down, when we speak to our children. Let us thank God for the blessed opportunity we have of sharing the joys and trials of each day with our children while they are still young, to spread peace and wisdom when they fight, to offer a shoulder when they cry, and to share the excitement of their discoveries and the joy of their accomplishments. As homeschoolers, we have the unique privilege of participating in so many moments of our children's lives. Let us thank God for this privilege and beg Him for the grace and prudence to spend this precious time wisely, to live in the present, and to fully treasure each moment He gives us with them.

# 27

## HOMESCHOOLING ON A TIGHT BUDGET

*"The real advantage of poverty lies in this: it
makes us raise our hearts to God."*

—ST. VINCENT DE PAUL

MANY homeschooling families struggle to keep
within a budget. Although homeschooling is far
less expensive than a parochial school, it costs much more
than a public school, and of course since we're teaching the
children all day, we're not bringing in extra income. Trying
to earn money at home in addition to homeschooling can
be stressful and exhausting, although it works for some
families. How can we afford curricula, books, maps,
puzzles, science and craft supplies, and field trips, in
addition to the regular household expenses? We yearn to
buy healthful food, the best curricula we can find, and
Catholic books and resources, yet such items cost so much
money. What can we do?

Here are a few practical and spiritual suggestions to
help keep expenses down.

We can buy used books. Abe.com, Amazon.com, and eBay are great resources for even the hardest-to-find books. If the book we want is too pricy at first, we can keep an eye on it; sometimes the price comes down if we wait a few months. We can find used books sales in our area through booksalefinder.com and buy books for only 25 or 50 cents a piece. (Videos, DVDs, CDs, and other items can also be bought secondhand from Amazon.com and eBay, and at many used book sales.) If we pick up interesting books on history, science, geography, or math when we see them, we can pull them out as needed, and we may never have to pore over expensive textbooks in curriculum catalogs.

We can use the local library. If our library doesn't have a book we want, we can request it through interlibrary loan. We can also borrow videos, DVDs, CDs, and magazines.

We can go to yard sales. The classifieds in Saturday morning papers will list local yard sales and give an idea of what types of items will be for sale. Generally, we need to go to a lot of yard sales, because one sale may have absolutely nothing we need—but if we go to enough, we'll eventually find things we need or want for our family. Community yard sales will obviously be worth a longer drive because of the larger selection. Children's toys, books, games, and clothes can often be bought at very low prices at yard sales. Children don't mind receiving second-hand birthday or Christmas gifts as long as they still function properly. Of course, at used book sales and yard sales, we need to make snap decisions, and we may not always have enough time to consider our purchase prudently. Other times, we may be tempted to buy something we don't need because it's such a great deal. We need to consider each purchase as practically and objectively as possible before we decide. Also, sometimes we'll buy something that's not in as good a shape as we thought, or doesn't quite fit right. Mistakes are a part of yard sale shopping, but generally, we save so much on the purchases that we *do* use that it's worth the few dollars wasted on misjudgments. To minimize mistakes, we can ask our Guardian Angel to guide us to whatever purchases will most benefit us and our families.

If we can't find an item that we want at a yard sale, we can try looking in the classifieds of our local paper or on eBay or Craigslist. By investing a little time and effort, we may be able to save a lot of money.

With a little creativity, we can invent our own educational games or science kits. Our children may learn more from helping to design the game or the kit than they would if we had bought it. As mentioned before, buying a used set of encyclopedias at a yard sale or book sale can provide a slew of pictures that make our home-made board games or card games look much more professional and appealing. Laminating the cards or board will ensure that they last longer. Furthermore, the product we create will be a precious family keepsake, more meaningful and more fun to use because it is the fruit of our labor.

All of these techniques require planning and shopping ahead of time, but if we are willing to put in the time, our budgets will benefit. When we do need something in a hurry, thrift shops will have a more consistent selection than yard sales, although the prices will be higher.

When we do decide to spend the money on something brand new, sometimes our school- and gift-shopping can overlap. We can give books, educational games, science kits, or craft supplies for Christmas or birthday presents if we think our children will enjoy them. Some book stores and craft stores offer discounts for teachers that extend to homeschoolers; a membership card to a homeschooling organization or some paperwork from our school district should be sufficient for proof that we homeschool, which we will need to bring to the store when we shop. If we decide to splurge on something new, we should research the product before buying. The Internet often features reviews of products or sample pages that can help us make decisions we won't regret.

Likewise, we need to choose field trips carefully. Many museum and zoo admission prices are exorbitant, but sometimes libraries offer discounts or free passes, and some museums are free on Sundays. Sometimes festivals celebrating local history are more affordable than museums, while being just as fun and educational. Many Christian churches offer free or inexpensive concerts of classical or jazz music. Local high schools or colleges might produce family-friendly plays with low ticket prices. Most towns have free outdoor concerts during the summer. (We can check out the summer concerts of all the surrounding towns, not just our own.) Berry-picking in the summer can be another inexpensive field trip if we live near pick-your-own berry farms. We can do research and find resources we never dreamed existed. If we don't have the Internet at home, we can research some of these resources at the local library, where Internet access is free.

Regarding healthful eating, we need to sit down and decide what our priorities are. Most of us can't afford to buy all-organic vegetables, fruit, and meat products, as well as whole-grain cereals, breads, pasta, and crackers, and completely avoid all products with high fructose corn syrup, MSG, genetically modified foods, and so forth. Where do we draw the line so our family can eat healthful meals without straining the budget? We need to do some research and decide what our priorities are so we can leave the grocery store each week without feeling guilt-ridden either over our unhealthy choices or our budgetary lapses. If we eat meat less often, we may be able to afford more fresh vegetables and fruit. Fruits or vegetables with thick skins, such as watermelon, are less likely to be affected by pesticides, and may be less harmful than other non-organic foods. Local farms or farmers' markets often sell fresh, naturally grown produce at competitive prices (and we'll have the satisfaction of supporting local family farms). If we have a yard, we could even grow some of our own fruit and vegetables, thus combining science class and home economics!

We can find meatless recipes in cookbooks at the library or online. Often, garbanzo beans or some other legume can be substituted for meat in a casserole or in tacos, providing the protein at significantly lower cost and without the worry of added antibiotics or hormones. We can avoid highly processed convenience food and junk food, which is both unhealthy and expensive, and try to buy at least some whole grains. Baking from scratch does not take much more time than using a box mix. Hot cereal, such as oatmeal, is often cheaper than cold, and many hot cereals are whole grain. We can buy a bread machine at a yard sale and bake our own bread without preservatives or high fructose corn syrup. We can stock up on meat that's free of antibiotics and hormones when it's on sale. We can cut out soda and substitute water, herbal tea, or unsweetened juice.

We can find recipes online to make our own healthy toothpaste, shampoo, laundry detergent, or deodorant. Baking soda mixed with water and a few drops of peppermint oil makes an inexpensive, all-natural toothpaste; grated Ivory soap melted in boiling water with some baking soda, salt, and essential oil like lavender or thyme oil makes an inexpensive laundry detergent that needs just a little wire whisk action before using. (Borax can be used instead of soap, but it is more likely to irritate sensitive skin.) Shampoo can also be made with grated Ivory soap melted in hot water, with a little jojoba oil and rosemary oil added to help prevent tangles, dandruff, and hair loss. Many people make their own deodorant with extra virgin coconut oil and a few drops of lemon oil or lavender oil, although we may need to be careful that it doesn't stain clothes. Felted yarn balls can be used in the dryer instead of dryer sheets to prevent clingy clothes; again, we can check the Internet for directions.

Over time, we'll find that we have to compromise between the multiple demands of health, time, taste, and finance. For example, during times of great stress, such as the first few months of pregnancy, or right after having a baby, or when there is illness in the family, we may need to buy some convenience foods until we have time to cook again. The key is to find a balance. We must be responsible stewards of the bodies God has given us, while keeping in mind that the body will die and the soul will not. We must not neglect the emotional and spiritual needs of our children because we want to make everything from scratch, nor should we allow ourselves to become stressed and agitated because we are trying to live up to an impossible ideal of nutritious cooking. Many homeschooling mothers will not be able to find time for educating their children, taking care of all the housework, and also growing a garden and baking fresh bread every day. Mothers with small children may not be able to do as much as those of us with older children who can help out more. We do not want to become cranky mothers who never have time to sing or play with their children just so we can provide the most healthful food possible. Therefore, while we try to nourish our children with good food, let us not make health an idol in our home, but concentrate our greatest efforts on nourishing the minds and souls God has entrusted to us.

Some of these cost-cutting techniques will involve sacrifices; whole grains or generic foods may seem bland after name brand, sugary foods. But we are not trying to raise hedonists. We're trying to raise saints, and we're trying to become saints ourselves. Sacrificing soda or junk food or meat can purify our hearts of our natural cravings for earthly comforts and pleasures and lead us to seek spiritual joys. Spiritual joys seem dry to us when we're steeped in physical comforts. But when those pleasures are taken away and we turn to prayer, meditation, and service to others, we realize that the spiritual life holds much greater and deeper joys. Slowly, and perhaps reluctantly, our children will learn these lessons, too. Becoming less concerned with self, and more focused on God and others, they will gradually develop into happy, prayerful, and self-sacrificing Christians.

# 28

## HOMESCHOOLING A
## LARGE FAMILY

*"He was our answer to the weak-hearted,
those afraid of life; more, he was our
answer to our own fears. We placed little
Joseph John Beardsley and his future into
the hands of the Lord with faith that was a
reflection of Abraham's. By all the rules of our
time and society we should have been afraid.
We had by any modern standards too many
children to support and raise properly. Now
we had another. Joseph John Beardsley was the
greatest act of faith we could perform."*

—HELEN BEARDSLEY

HELEN Beardsley was a widow with eight children who married a widower with ten children. They went on to have two more children together. She wrote the story of her unusual, and sometimes amusing, situation, in her book, *Who Gets the Drumstick?*, an inspiring testimony of human struggle over sorrow and fear, and ultimately, the triumph of faith and love. Her frank admission of her own anxieties, which were conquered by her faith in God, may reflect the feelings of many mothers who have fewer children in an age that frowns on large families.

And if raising a large family can be intimidating, how much more so is it to homeschool a large family!

Obviously, organization and time management are crucial. Just a little thing like planning a weekly meal schedule, for example, can help each day proceed more smoothly. Setting general goals at the beginning of the week and even at the start of each day can help us figure out what needs to be done and when we're going to fit it in. This would include anything outside the normal daily schedule, such as weekly cleaning and vacuuming, and any projects, crafts, experiments, or outings that we need to set aside some time for. We can also keep a list of little tasks that need to be done, so whenever we have a free moment, we can sew on that button or write that thank you note, instead of letting those precious moments go to waste.

Delegating household chores, of course, is vital to avoid burnout. While children may sigh or complain about helping out, being responsible for household chores builds self-discipline, self-esteem, and habits of industry.

Another strategy is to combine lessons when possible. Children in different grades can study the same historical time period or science topics; the older children can read books slightly below their reading level in history or science as long as the information presented is new; in fact, they may be able to process difficult concepts better if the reading level is not challenging to them. An older child could also receive a beneficial review of math facts by playing a math game with a younger sibling. Lessons are more fun when done together, and combined lessons require less time and effort from us.

Training our children to do schoolwork independently can also assist us tremendously. We can make up a list of tasks for each day so each child can start and possibly even finish their lessons without us, coming to us only if they have a question or when they need us to check their work. Once a child has learned to read proficiently, history and science can be done with very little help. We could discuss what they've been reading over lunch or while we're nursing the baby, and we can set aside one day a week to do science experiments or a timeline together, or some other hands-on projects. Allowing the child to choose crafts or activities and come to us only if they need help can free us from unnecessary stress. There's no need to feel guilty about arranging for our children to do the majority of their lessons without us. Working independently builds self-discipline, responsibility, and independence, as well as preparing them for college and for many careers. We just need to check their work regularly to make sure they are doing it; even otherwise docile, obedient children can succumb to the temptation of skipping assignments or doing assignments carelessly if their work is never checked.

We must try not to allow feelings of guilt to engulf us as mothers of large families. We have an enormous job, and we feel pulled in so many directions at once; at any given moment one child may be asking us to read to him, another calling she's done on the potty, a third waiting for us to correct his math, all the while the baby is crying to be fed, baskets of laundry are blocking the doorways, and we hear a full-scale argument going on upstairs. How can we tend to the needs of each child, accomplish all the housework, and remain calm? Don't we all hear a voice in the back of our heads accusing us of neglecting someone or something? Are we sometimes tempted to wonder if we have we bitten off more than we can chew?

The strategies suggested above should assist us, but no matter how well-organized we are, there will always be something we didn't quite get to—a toddler who wasn't read to today, a science project that's been put on the back burner for a month, bed sheets that haven't been washed— there's always something. We mustn't allow guilt to over- whelm us, because in giving our children many sisters and brothers, we are giving them a gift that never ends, a gift that far surpasses all the other little things that we wish we had time to do for them but do not. With each new sibling we give our children playmates, lifelong friends, and daily opportunities for unselfish giving. Moreover, our children have the unique chance to learn about relationships—how to get along with different personalities, how to speak tactfully, how to persuade convincingly, how to argue fairly, how to apologize humbly, and how to forgive graciously. They learn to accept others' faults and to work with others' weaknesses, to help each other, to share with each other, and to compromise with each other. These lessons are not learned quickly or quietly, but they will yield a wisdom and tact that will serve them well in all their relationships for the rest of their lives.

In fact, being too busy to hover over each child all the time and to solve every little problem can be an advantage: children learn to solve problems, including disagreements, on their own and to help each other. They become more self-reliant and self-confident. Isn't that what we are all striving to raise our children to be?

Furthermore, children often learn more from games or experiments or reading they initiate themselves than from experiences that we plan for them. Sometimes we may dream wistfully of the beautifully detailed, hands-on lesson plans we would create if we had fewer children and more time—each lesson complete with coordinating readings, crafts, and field trips. But although this dream might satisfy a desire to be the perfect teacher, would our schemes really enable our children to learn better? In reality, children learn a tremendous amount from their own unstructured play or self-guided projects .We may consider their activities unsophisticated, messy, and uneducational, but we're forgetting that children learn best when they are fully engaged—intellect, emotions, and will. It is then that they experience their most meaningful discoveries, their true "eureka" moments. We may not always be able to see that learning is occurring, and they may not always be able to tell us in words what gems they have gleaned, but during their free, unstructured time, they are learning in the truest sense of the word. Do we need to feel guilty for allowing them time for activities like these?

In a big family, we do need to make sure each child receives the love and attention he needs. We can take turns playing a game with each child, letting them help us make dinner, or taking them with us to get groceries or out for an ice cream. But we needn't feel guilty over all that we can't do, for with every sibling we've given to our children, we've given them untold opportunities to learn, as well as a friendship that may last them the rest of their lives.

# 29

## HOMESCHOOLING TODDLERS, PRE-SCHOOLERS, AND KINDERGARTENERS

*"Every mother is like Moses.*
*She does not enter the promised land.*
*She prepares a world she will not see."*

—POPE PAUL VI

ONE of the most common questions from beginning homeschoolers is how to keep their toddlers and pre-schoolers busy while they do lessons with the older children. The best answer to this question is that the situation does become easier. The first few years are definitely the hardest! After we establish a routine of doing lessons in the morning with the older ones, the younger ones will begin to understand that their time will come later and will learn to play quietly by themselves. As we continue to have more babies, they will generally fall into the pattern that has already been established with much less effort. In order to train our little ones to play quietly and not interrupt lessons, we can assure them that they will get their turn with us, but only if they behave well during the older children's lessons. Then, after we're done with the older ones, we must be sure to sit down and read to the little ones or play a game with them. Sometimes we may want to hold little ones on our lap while we do lessons with the older children; but once our attention becomes focused on removing pencils or school papers from the toddler's curious hands, then we need to put the toddler down so we can focus on the child we're helping with lessons. If some of the older children finish their lessons early, they could also help by watching or playing with the toddlers so we can spend some uninterrupted time with one of the other children.

Of course, when our little ones see us spending time working with the older children on lessons, they may beg to do some lessons, too. While there is no reason to pressure our child into structured lessons at a young age, our little ones may enjoy some simple activities, according to their abilities. We can find some very easy maze or dot-to-dot books at doverpublications.com, at the local parent-teacher store, or sometimes even at a craft store. We could also make some activity sheets on our own. For example, we can draw some triangles on a piece of paper, write the numbers one through ten at the bottom of the page, have the child count how many triangles there are, and then circle that number. Such simple activities are fun, and they develop fine motor skills and counting skills. We can also show our child how to print the letters of the alphabet or to match each letter with a picture of a word that begins with that letter. We can end our lesson by reading a story from a Catholic children's Bible. This will enable us to make our way through the Bible systematically over and over so that our child will gradually become familiar with all the major Bible stories.

Of course, these little activities will not constitute the full extent of our teaching. Apart from formal lessons, we should read engaging picture books appropriate for the child's attention span, including alphabet books or counting books if the child is interested. We can play simple games with them, such as animal lotto, Go Fish, or Memory. It's also important to sing songs with our child and talk to our child, asking him questions, listening attentively, and answering the questions he asks. Providing simple puzzles and, even more importantly, some kind of building blocks, will also promote learning on many different levels for our toddler. Moreover, we must say morning and night prayers with him, tell stories about Jesus and the saints, and encourage him to thank God for pleasant things that happen during the day and to offer unpleasant things up in union with Christ on the cross. We need to explain to our child that we can't always prevent him from getting hurt, but by reminding him to offer the hurt up, we are helping him to use his hurt to do good for others. When we offer our pain to Jesus bravely, He can see how much we love Him, and our offering becomes a prayer that can help the souls in Purgatory or convert sinners. We should be sure to tell our children that we can offer our fun and happy times up to Jesus, too; but because it's harder to offer hurts up cheerfully, offering up our hurts shows our love more. Our child will probably learn more about God and the world he lives in from our reading, playing, and chatting than he will from his little activities, if we make a real effort to talk to him while we dress him, bathe him, and eat with him, and not spend that time talking over his head to his older siblings or to friends on the phone.

When we take our children to Mass, we can remind all of them, but especially the young ones, that the little round Host they will see looks like a small piece of flat, white, bread but is really the Body and Blood of Jesus. If our little one sits next to us at Mass, we can nudge him at the elevation or even whisper softly in his ear, "That's Jesus" or "I love You, Jesus!" This sacrament holds great wonder for little ones when they are told, outside of Mass, "When you love someone, you want to be near them, as close as possible. Jesus loves you so much that He wants to be as close to you as He possibly can, so He made Himself look like bread so He can come right inside of you. You're too little to receive Him yet, but He is so happy when you come to visit Him, and He's looking forward to the day when He can come right inside you. If you want to receive Him, tell Him so. It will make Him so happy to know that you want to be close to Him, too." The idea of someone as important as Jesus waiting for them and longing to be with them will fill children with a feeling of affection in return. We can bring even the very littlest ones to church during the week when no one is there except Jesus in the tabernacle. This is a wonderful opportunity to walk around the church, telling our little ones about the statues and stained glass windows there, and especially about the special gold box up front that we call the tabernacle where Jesus waits so patiently for them to visit Him.

Many books have been written about the numerous games and activities we can do with our little ones. Which activities we choose is not important. The main thing is not to overlook these youngsters in our efforts to do science experiments or field trips or other "important" projects with the older children. The innocence and charm of this age vanishes so quickly, and we will always look back with regret if we haven't spent plenty of quality time with our pre-schoolers. It was probably a little child like this of whom Our Lord said, "Of such is the kingdom of God" (Mark 10:14).

# 30

## HOMESCHOOLING BOYS

*"Education today makes no difference*
*between the training of man and woman.*
*This is right from the point of view of*
*opportunities that are open to both; but*
*it is short-sighted when one considers the*
*psychological differences between the two."*
—ARCHBISHOP FULTON J. SHEEN

APART from concerns about the moral content and politically correct agenda of the curricula used in public schools, having a son is one of the most powerful reasons to homeschool. Many educational experts contend that the female-dominated school system does grave disservice to male students, requiring them to adapt to a structured environment before they are emotionally ready, demanding that they sit still for inappropriately long periods of time, and instructing them in a style that is unconsciously geared for a female brain.

Since boys do mature more slowly than girls, why are boys required to start school at the same age as girls?

Attending school at too young an age can result in low self-esteem and frustration when the child is unable to adapt to the structured environment and learn concepts above his age level. Studies tell us that this low self-esteem and academic frustration can, in turn, lead to low grades and juvenile delinquency throughout the school years, even as far as high school. High school AP classes and National Honor Societies have a disproportionate ratio of girls to boys, and now more women are going on for college and higher degrees than men. Furthermore, most boys need more physical activity than most girls, and requiring them to sit at a desk for the bulk of a school day and then come home to do a few hours' worth of homework can only be termed unwholesome, even cruel, treatment. Lastly, learning in a classroom setting with little individual attention, taught by a teacher who is usually a woman, using curricula and lesson plans designed primarily by women, can result in boys struggling with material because the mode of presentation is foreign and inimical. Boys think differently from girls, they process information differently, and they learn to articulate differently; only a rare teacher can make up for this difference in a classroom setting.

Many little girls enjoy sedentary occupations and find a certain satisfaction in filling out worksheets, coloring pictures, and following a teacher's directions. They enjoy reading cute little stories about girls playing with dolls or putting on a play. Most boys tend to be non-conformists—trailblazers and explorers—at heart. They don't want to be bothered with filling out sheets or coloring neatly or reading silly stories about other boys playing cowboys. A book must be compelling—truly informative or exciting—to interest boys. Otherwise, they'd rather be up doing something active, like making paper dinosaurs, ramming matchbox cars into each other, running, jumping, or building. When required to sit still and process information, they will either struggle in their efforts to learn and grow discouraged, or they will be suffocated with boredom; either way, the temptation to rebel and give up studying will be strong. As Hilaire Belloc said, "All men have an instinct for conflict: at least, all healthy men," and what are boys but men in the making?

Author Michael Gurian scientifically explains how conventional schools shortchange boys in his eye-opening book, *Boys and Girls Learn Differently*. Although he never draws the obvious conclusion that homeschooling is a preferred method for educating boys, many of his findings on the differences between boys' and girls' brains are quite fascinating. Even more helpful are Leonard Sax's books, *Why Gender Matters* and *Boys Adrift*, which demonstrate the differences between boys and girls in an even more practical manner. Although we will not agree with Sax's condoning of homosexuality, his other insights will prove invaluable for us in our endeavors to understand our sons.

With all of this in mind, we can be glad that we have decided to homeschool our boys, for a homeschool is naturally less prone to have the faults that put boys at a disadvantage. Still, we must be careful to educate our boys according to their needs and not our own preconceived notions. We must remember boys develop more slowly than girls and refrain from comparing their achievements with those of their sisters when they were the same age. We must be patient and wait to teach them to read only when they express an interest, without pressuring or nagging them. We can allow them to lay aside dull readers and find books on astronauts or dinosaurs or knights or some other topic that really interests them. (The old *Cowboy Sam* or *Dan Frontier* readers are interesting to boys, if we can find them. There are also plenty of easy reader books on dinosaurs.) We can avoid giving them a schedule that is too rigidly structured; although all children need a daily routine, undue rigidity will reap restlessness, boredom, and apathy. We can implement a more hands-on approach to help children grasp concepts on more than one level. Boys also need to be allowed to be active during the day, and to be shown the relevance of what they're learning. When boys are not motivated to learn, they will stumble along at a barely perceptible speed; when boys are motivated, they will soar far ahead of our expectations.

Yes, most of the time we mothers do the majority of the homeschooling, but this does not necessarily put our sons at a disadvantage. True, we can't help looking at the world from a female perspective and approaching lessons with a female mind, but because we'll be teaching our sons one-on-one, we can be sensitive to their needs and learning styles and adapt our lessons accordingly. We can be attentive to our sons as we explain concepts in different ways, to see what methods seem to work most effectively. We can allow our sons plenty of exercise and minimal paper work, and encourage them to tackle meaningful projects that will motivate them as they learn.

The more we read about the development of boys and attend to our own sons' needs, the better we will be able to create a learning environment that will maximize our sons' talents and strengthen their weaknesses. Then we can thank God for our opportunity to raise virtuous, virile, unstifled, and motivated Catholic men.

# 31

## HOMESCHOOLING GIRLS

*"People talk of the pathos and failure*
*of plain women; but it is a more terrible thing*
*that a beautiful woman may succeed*
*in everything but womanhood."*

— G. K. CHESTERTON

ONE of the advantages of homeschooling our girls is that we have the power to keep them pure and free from the unhealthy influences of today's culture. Our society's concept of womanhood is quite different from the Christian concept. From the time our girls are small, our culture tries to push impossibly tiny-waisted and large-busted Barbies at them with tight-fitting, trendy clothes. As our girls grow older, clothes in stores all seem to become tighter and so clingy that they reveal all the contours of a girl's changing body. Young girls even wear make-up, unable to believe that God made them beautiful, just as they are. Many develop eating disorders or low self-esteem because their figures don't match the surgically produced, airbrushed figures of the models they see in magazines.

Girls today go to great pains to make themselves beautiful and attractive, but all they succeed in doing is making themselves look like sexual objects.

This is the scenario we hope to protect our daughters from. We want them to understand the glory of their femininity. The true glory of woman is her ability to bring forth life. The hormones that enable us to realize physical motherhood also provide the emotional and spiritual attraction for mothering others, whether as teachers, nurses, aunts, or in some other capacity. Even women who enter the religious life or remain single often experience spiritual motherhood. Motherhood, as we mothers know, is a vocation of self-sacrifice; our monthly periods can cause emotional upheaval and physical discomfort; pregnancy brings both emotional and physical hardships to an entirely new level, culminating in childbirth; and then follows breastfeeding the baby and taking care of his every need as he grows, which requires a lifetime of selflessness and love. Furthermore, our bodies are weaker and our emotions are more variable than a man's because this better prepares us for the life of love and nurturing that usually falls to us. Our job is not usually to make our way in the world, to explore, to compete, to conquer, and to build; our job is to nourish, physically, emotionally, and spiritually, those vulnerable lives placed in our care. Yes, some women's lives take them outside of the home and into the world of men, but these are the exception, not the rule—or they would be, if women today took more seriously their responsibility to raise their children themselves. (This is not to disparage mothers who make the sacrifice to work outside the home due to real monetary need. However, the number of mothers who work outside the home has gone far beyond these few who work so their families can afford basic needs, rather than luxuries.) The work that has traditionally belonged to women does not degrade us—on the contrary, it ennobles us. In many ways, the woman's vocation is purer and higher than a man's, for a woman's life is spent on polishing jewels that will never die or decay—the jewels of her children's souls. Men work for money, and that is necessary, for we must eat; but women labor for the souls of their children. Because this vocation keeps us primarily in our homes, women have traditionally been known as purer and nobler than men, not sullied by the vulgar language and underhanded dealings of the business or political world. Men who had to spend their working hours in a corrupt society could come home and be reminded of higher things—piety, purity, innocence, and love.

For this reason, women have traditionally dressed differently from men. Our bodies are different, our roles in life are different, and our clothes should reflect that difference. Women are set apart from the world, set apart so that every man can come home to a haven of purity and goodness. Our clothes remind men of the respect they feel toward us, not only because of our weakness, but also because of our strength, our unique ability to bear new life, new souls destined to praise God forever in heaven—the most fragile and vulnerable members of society—in our very bodies.

Sadly, with the advent of the radio, the television, and the Internet, the home is no longer the haven of innocence that women used to make it. Also, it has gone out of fashion for women to wear dresses or skirts every day. However, women who still wear skirts report that they feel more confident, more feminine, and more respected by the men they chance to meet. Isn't this part of the femininity that we want to pass on to our daughters? Our clothes reflect how we feel about ourselves. If our daughters wear the tight-fitting, low-cut, or clingy clothes that are usually found in the stores, then they will think of themselves as—and even start acting like—sexual objects. Hasn't this happened in our society today, where teen cohabitation, unwed pregnancies, and abortions have skyrocketed? On the other hand, if our daughters dress in pants or shorts, they will have the tendency to act like men. And what women really wants to boss her husband around—literally, "to wear the pants in the household"—or to be the bread-winner while someone else watches her children? Again, that is what is happening today. Just by dressing modestly and wearing a skirt, our daughters are sending a message to everyone around them. Often, other people will curb their vulgar language or apologize for it when in the presence of a truly feminine woman; men will be more likely to open the door for her, and boys will be far less likely to ask her out for a one-night stand.

Modesty is a difficult issue to talk to our teens about. Teenaged girls are notoriously emotional and sensitive about their clothes and their appearance, even though homeschooling removes them from the arena of peer pressure that exists in high schools today. We may find Colleen Hammond's *Dressing With Dignity* a great boon in helping us explain to our daughters why we should dress modestly, and in finding sources for modest clothes if we don't sew our own. Impurity in movies, television shows, songs, websites, and common conversation is a tremendous problem in today's world, but by dressing modestly, our girls will be part of the solution, and their modesty will also protect them, to some extent, from the impurity of the world.

In addition to dressing modestly, we can encourage our daughters not to wear make-up. Our daughters are beautiful the way God made them. We must reinforce that. The purity and beauty of an unmade-up face far surpasses the hollow sophistication and false security that make-up offers. Let our girls enhance their beauty by learning to do their hair in different styles, adorning their hair with ribbons and bows and wearing attractive but modest dresses. A necklace or a pair of earrings can add a little color or style to an otherwise plain outfit. All of these things accent the mystery of a girl's femininity and allow the glory of her budding womanhood to shine through, whereas immodest clothes debase her, and make-up actually masks the beauty she was born with.

Yes, it is difficult to find modest clothes. Fortunately, if we can't find much in the retail stores, we can try thrift shops, which often sell clothing that was made before the immodest trends became so prevalent; we can also shop on-line for more conservative styles. *Dressing With Dignity* has a good list of such websites, or we can try searching on our own, with a little prayer to St. Maria Goretti, the patron saint of teen-aged girls. Of course, we should set an example of wearing modest, feminine clothes and feeling confident in the beauty that God gave us by going without make-up. This will be the most powerful teacher of all. If we are determined, we can raise chaste, feminine daughters who thank God for the blessed honor of being women.

# 32

## HOMESCHOOLING TEENS

*". . . [T]hose who in your presence are not*
*ashamed to make use of scandalous words,*
*and expressions of double meaning.*
*Those who grumble, tell lies, swear, blaspheme;*
*those who try to keep you away from church,*
*want you to steal, disobey your parents*
*and superiors or to neglect your duty.*
*With tears in my eyes, I beseech you to keep*
*far away from such companions."*

—ST. JOHN BOSCO

HOMESCHOOLING through high school presents unique challenges that intimidate many would-be homeschoolers. But moral and spiritual formation during the teen years is far too important to be left to the teachers and classmates of a local school. Teens are emotional and sensitive, engaged in the confusing and often painful process of discovering their self-identity and slowly learning independence in many different spheres. They are beginning to seek reasons behind their beliefs and to develop their own opinions on philosophy, politics, and literature. They are becoming more interested in the opposite sex and considering what qualities they desire in a spouse. In short, they are budding adults.

Do we want to subject our children at this critical, vulnerable stage in their lives to the influence of peer pressure, a culture of drugs and sexual promiscuity among classmates, and politically correct, often relativistic or atheistic, teachers? Sadly, Catholic high schools are only a little better in these respects than public schools. Is participation in a chemistry lab or a calculus class worth the price of submitting our child to the pernicious atmosphere that permeates most high schools? Are the teenagers produced by our society such paragons of intellect, culture, virtue, modesty, and maturity that we want our teens to mature like them? If we spend an hour listening unobtrusively to some high school students hanging out at the local library or convenient store, we'll know exactly what kind of language and conversation our teen will encounter on a daily basis at school, and our decision will probably be made right then and there.

Teenagers do not need to go through a stage of rebellion, such as we see in so many families in our society. In an interview for HSLDA's *The Court Report*, Dr. Robert Epstein explained that other cultures do not experience the problem of juvenile delinquency and teenage rebellion that our modern Western society does, because other cultures treat young adults with respect and consideration for their blossoming powers by granting them increasing freedom and responsibility. Even in the not-so-distant past in the United States, teens were allowed to quit school, get a job, and even marry. While we may not want our teenagers marrying, we should not prolong their childhood longer than necessary. We must respect their need for growing independence. Homeschooling allows us the freedom and flexibility to do this.

Homeschooled teens can do a great deal of schoolwork on their own, spending much less time on their studies than teens in conventional schools, and their extra time can be used to develop skills or learn information pertinent to their own interests and potential careers. Part-time jobs, apprenticeships, and volunteer opportunities can provide valuable experience in a field of their choice, while helping teens earn money for college or a car. Such opportunities may help our teen determine if a certain field really appeals to him as a future job; if it doesn't, he can go on to research another field that may hold more interest. He could earn money by tutoring other homeschoolers in music lessons, carpentry, or some other area in which he excels. Teens can also be given more responsibility around the house, helping out with housework, yard work, babysitting, or a home business. This makes teens feel useful and needed, as opposed to spending all their time on academics, which can often appear dull and meaningless. For instance, a teen who is planning on a career as a journalist may become irritated and restless at spending exorbitant amounts of time on physics or algebra problems. Independent study gives a teen more time to develop his talents and to develop practical skills like cooking, sewing, changing a light bulb, or fixing a broken radio. He may even want to try to start a small home business himself, thus gaining priceless entrepreneurial experience from the safety of home. These activities will give the teen self-confidence and a sense of purpose, besides preparing him more effectively for the real world.

Of course, in high school we do have to follow certain standards if we want our children to graduate according to the standards of our state or be accepted by a college or a trade school—or even if we simply want to raise cultured, well-informed adults. We may have to implement more structure than we've used in the past, but we still do not need to espouse the rigid methodology of conventional schools. We must consider our child's talents and needs. If our teen has a strong scientific bent, we may want to invest in a higher quality, in-depth science program, while this may not be necessary for a child with more literary proclivities. All teens need to learn both science and literature, but our approach and emphasis will be different for each child. If we feel higher math and science are beyond our ability to teach, we may consider enrolling our child in a correspondence course that offers a telephone line for questions, or finding an appropriate online course, or we can enroll our teen in a local community college for those courses. Or we could pay another homeschooling parent with an expertise in math or science to tutor our child. If none of these options appeals to us, then we can fall back on our original methodology of using living books, which can boost our child's interest in and comprehension of complex material.

There are living books available on such unlikely subjects as pre-algebra, algebra, geometry, calculus, biology, chemistry, and physics, which may prove invaluable to a family that does not want to suddenly change their whole style of homeschooling in the upper grades. Living books are not only more interesting, but they're also far less expensive than traditional high school textbooks. The lower cost makes high school more affordable, while allowing us the flexibility of switching books during the year if our child has trouble with the teaching method of the book we've chosen. Polka Dot Publishing puts out the *Life of Fred* series by Stanley F. Schmidt, which teaches upper level math in such a way as to entice both students who hate math, and students who love it. (He has more recently written math books for elementary school children as well.) Other choices for high school math might include *A + Notes for Beginning Algebra* by Rong Yang, *Homework Helpers: Algebra* by Denise Szecsei or *The Algebra Survival Guide*, with the accompanying workbook, by Josh Rappaport. We can devise an enjoyable course on economics with either *Economics in One Lesson* by Henry Hazlitt or *Whatever Happened to Penny Candy?* by Richard Maybury or *Economics for Helen* by Hilaire Belloc. For students who need another year of math but don't want to go into calculus, a good book on consumer math or statistics could fit the bill.

John Hudson Tiner's books, *Exploring the World of Biology*, *Exploring the World of Chemistry*, and *Exploring the World of Physics*, would be excellent source for a junior high science program; these books, written from a Christian perspective, are fun, informative, living books on science. They could even be used as a base for a high school science course if amply supplemented by more in-depth sources. (Tiner also has a superb book on math, *Exploring the World of Mathematics*, to intrigue junior high math students.) For a more comprehensive high school curriculum, we could try titles like: *Homework Helpers: Chemistry* and *Homework Helpers: Physics*, both by Greg Curran; *Basic Physics: A Self-Teaching Guide* by Karl F. Kuhn; *For the Love of Physics* by Walter Lewin; *Chemistry for Everyone* by Suzanne Lahl; or *Chemistry: Concepts and Problems: A Self-Teaching Guide* by Clifford C. Houk. Once we've chosen a good chemistry book to use as a foundation, we can supplement inexpensively with more living books, such as *The Chemical History of a Candle* by Michael Faraday; *Chemistry for Every Kid* by Janice VanCleave; or *The Mystery of the Periodic Table* by Benjamin Wiker (all in print). Alvin and Virginia Silverstein have written several books on various topics in biology, which, though not from a Christian perspective, would prove informative and interesting, including *The Code of Life* (as long as we discuss the last chapter on genetic engineering with our child) and *Cells: Building Blocks of Life*, as well as many more titles. In addition, some teens might enjoy the illuminating discussions on the relation between science and religion that are found in Fr. Thomas Dubay's *The Evidential Power of Beauty* or the down-to-earth approach of Tom Bethell's *The Politically Incorrect Guide to Science*.

Doing a search on Amazon.com can help us find a wonderful array of living books on these and other traditional high school subjects, along with reviews by readers on the quality of each book. Equipment for upper level science classes, from microscopes to frogs for dissection, is available at homesciencetools.com, but less equipment will be needed with a less formal, living-books approach—and most teens will learn and retain more of what they learn. Furthermore, this style can make high school science affordable and more practical, especially for students not planning to make science their career, while teens with a truly scientific bent won't be held back by a rigid or restrictive curriculum, but will be free to learn about and experiment with whatever they are most interested in. This will mean, once again, a more effective method that allows each student to learn at his own pace and go as far as he desires to go.

We have spent extra time on science because many parents of teens hesitate to homeschool through high school primarily because they feel unequipped to teach advanced science, complete with complicated labs and expensive, high-tech equipment. However, we should realize that whether our children are planning a career in science or not, this kind of science class is not necessary—or even particularly desirable—for our children.

Literature is, for most parents, less intimidating than higher math and science. Nevertheless, we must realize the importance of ensuring that our children read the classics and understand them. While many literary guides interpret the classics according to the relativist, left-wing agenda so commonly found in academic circles today, we might be relieved to find that Ignatius Press is publishing a series of classics edited by Joseph Pearce, from *Hamlet* to *Pride and Prejudice* to *Dracula*, featuring essays by Catholic literary experts to help our teens truly understand the text in the way it was meant. Furthermore, Pearce's books on Shakespeare, *Quest for Shakespeare* (which examines Shakespeare's life and proves that he was a faithful Catholic) or *Through Shakespeare's Eyes* (which examines three of his plays in the light of Shakespeare's staunch Catholic faith during a severe persecution), should be read by every high school student who wants to truly understand Shakespeare's plays and the milieu in which they were written. Fans of *The Hobbit* may also enjoy *Bilbo's Journey* by Joseph Pearce, which explores the Christian meaning behind this popular book.

Lastly, we should also consider that teens may develop a strong desire to meet others of their age, outside their own family. We need to respect this need and fill it as best we can. The choice of companions at this impressionable age is as important as ever, so we must move carefully. We can see if our parish has any activities for teens, such as a CYO group – hopefully not just involving sports – and we can check local homeschooling groups as well. If our parish or homeschooling group does not have any activities for teens, we can always begin a group ourselves and see if any other teens join, advertising in our parish bulletin or homeschool newsletter. Starting a book club is an easy, non-intimidating way to begin. We can allow the teens to vote on the book, preferably a classic that can be found at the local library to keep expenses down. Then we can be present to help start stimulating conversations, keeping ourselves in the background as much as possible. The single most important thing we can do to foster any teen group might be to provide tasty refreshments. Other clubs we could start might be an apologetics club, a chess club, a knitting club, a scrabble club, a singing club (perhaps specializing in Gregorian chant or barbershop harmony, according to our teens' interest), a mixed martial arts club, and so forth. More ambitious teens may want to start a dramatic club that puts on short plays, possibly even plays written by one or two club members, or they may want to hold square dances, which is not only fun but great exercise. If we start off small and let our teenagers take most of the responsibility on their shoulders, we may be surprised at the success of our efforts.

If we really want what is best for our teenagers, we will continue to homeschool them in a learning environment suited to their needs, while respecting their growing desire for independence , responsibility and socialization. Above all, we will shower them with understanding and love as they struggle through the painful and challenging process of blossoming into adults.

# 33

## SELF-SACRIFICE

*"How sweet has it been to me to be
deprived of the delights of a frivolous world!
What incomparable joy have I felt after a
privation once so dreaded."*

—ST. AUGUSTINE

THE life of a mother is one of self-sacrifice. Our time and energy is completely devoted to the care of our youngsters, especially when they are little. As homeschoolers, however, this role of constant self-giving is extended, for not only do we continue to shoulder the responsibility of watching them all day, every day, during the week, but we also concern ourselves with every aspect of their education, which requires planning, preparation, and prayer. We must learn self-discipline to accomplish all that we need to do each day, and we may even decide to give up a certain kind of music or a way of dressing that we do not want to pass on to our children. Our work is rewarding, as we watch our children grow and develop into virtuous, cultured, adults, but there are times when we feel too frustrated or tired or discouraged to appreciate the rewards of our vocation.

There are both practical and spiritual remedies to help us through these difficult times. Obviously, getting time away from the children about once a week will refresh us— even if that time is spent at yard sales or book sales looking for gifts for them! Keeping up with a hobby, whether knitting, writing, drawing, sewing, scrapbooking, or painting, can also relax us and serve as a good model to our children as they work through projects of their own.

Another help is to write down all the funny things our children say or do, as well as their accomplishments or landmarks. These can be kept in a notebook (either a separate notebook for each child or one big one for everybody) and read over when we feel a bit jaded or annoyed with our offspring. Looking over a photo album of our children may have the same effect. Memories of our children at their cutest moments will warm our hearts and put our own discouragement in proper perspective; we'll realize that our time with our children is short, that difficult stages or annoying faults are passing, and that we must appreciate and cherish each child while we have the chance.

Ultimately, however, our inspiration in self-sacrifice must come from Christ, Who poured Himself out completely, even to the very last drop of His Blood. He did not complain when the Roman whips lacerated the skin of His back; so we must not complain when, exhausted from a long day, we sit down to rest only to be immediately summoned to resolve an argument or to change a diaper. And when we chance to enter our children's bedroom and find an unholy mess, we must not rant and rave or despair, but firmly tell our children to clean the mess up, remembering Christ's own forbearance with those who crucified Him. If He can be merciful and patient in great things, then surely we can be merciful and patient in little things. Children are a work in progress—saints in the making—and we must not expect perfection.

Isaiah says Christ "was offered because it was his own will, and he opened not his mouth. He shall be led as a sheep to the slaughter and shall be dumb as a lamb before his shearer, and he shall not open his mouth" (Isaiah 53:7). Do we imitate Christ's example? Or are our mouths always open to spew forth grumbling, complaining, and murmuring, ultimately rebelling against the wisdom and goodness of an omnipotent God Who has placed us in our specific situation, as mother to these particular children with these particular faults? What kind of sacrifice are we offering when we offer it with unwilling, resentful hearts?

Let us curb our rebellious inclinations and imitate our meek and mild Savior, Whose only comment in His agony was, "Not as I will, but as thou wilt." (Matthew 26:39). Let us treasure each fleeting moment that we share with our children, imperfect as both we and they are, and thank God for the life of each one, with all their little foibles, repeating over and over in our hearts, "Not as I will, but as thou wilt."

# 34

## NURTURING VOCATIONS TO THE PRIESTHOOD AND RELIGIOUS LIFE

*"Christ made my soul beautiful with
the jewels of grace and virtue.
I belong to Him whom the angels serve."*

—ST. AGNES

AS Catholic mothers, we can hope for no greater blessing than to have one or more of our children called by God to the priesthood or religious life. Such a calling requires a sacrifice on our part, as well as on the part of the child, but we will find that sons or daughters who make the ultimate sacrifice in giving themselves completely to the Lord are a source of abundant graces and joy that will last throughout our life.

How can we encourage our children to be open to a vocation to the priesthood or the religious life? Traditionally, most religious vocations have come from large families, primarily because children with many

225

siblings learn to share, help others, and make sacrifices as a natural part of daily life, so when the time comes to choose a career, a life of self-sacrifice is a natural, familiar choice for them. If God does not bless us with many children, we must try our best to find little, daily occasions for our children to share, to serve others, and to sacrifice. No matter how large or small our family is, we have a tendency to want to do things for our children or give things to them because we love them, and we must temper these inclinations with a higher love—a love of their souls. We must avoid spoiling our children by buying them everything that we can afford; we must let them occasionally make their own or do without. In choosing food, we shouldn't always pander to their tastes, but prepare food that is inexpensive but wholesome. Although the children may grumble a lot at first, as time goes by, they will grow less spoiled and more appreciative of what they do have. For example, children who are used to having cold cereal every day will fuss when they find out they're having cornflakes again, but children who are fed hot cereal several times a week will be excited to see any cold cereal on the table, even cornflakes. We must take the seasons of Advent and Lent seriously and cut down sweets and other junk food, as well as using this time to have our children do some act of service every day, such as reading to a younger child, playing a game that another child chooses, or helping a sibling with a chore. Children with no siblings may have a harder time thinking of acts of service, but they can always help their parents with the housework. We can also look for opportunities for service in our neighborhood. Is there an elderly neighbor who might like a visit or some homemade cookies or some help around the house? Do we live near a mother with little children who might need some assistance with the little ones while she gets housework done or rests a little? Older children could babysit for free while the mother actually leaves the house to go shopping or to dine out with her husband. They could also shovel driveways for elderly neighbors, teach CCD at the parish, or take part in some pro-life work in the diocese. Obviously, works of mercy performed in our neighborhood or community will benefit children from families of any size.

Devotion to the Blessed Sacrament is another common hallmark of a vocation to the priesthood or religious life. After all, the priest's highest privilege is to change bread and wine into the Body and Blood of Christ during Mass, so if a boy has only minimal interest in the Blessed Sacrament, he will not feel much interest in the priesthood. Likewise, many religious attend daily Mass and spend an hour in front of the Blessed Sacrament every day; this is where they receive the strength and grace to fulfill their vocation, whether it be an active life of teaching or nursing, or a contemplative life of prayer and meditation. Therefore, we can try to take our children to daily Mass whenever possible, as well as on visits to the Blessed Sacrament. Boys can be encouraged to become altar servers, which is like an apprenticeship for the priesthood, while girls, if they are interested, could help wash or mend altar linens or volunteer at our parish in some other way.

Example is of prime importance in our families. Who are the heroes and heroines of our children? Actors? Singers? Athletes? While there's nothing wrong with enjoying a good movie or beautiful music or an exciting sports event, and admiring the skill of those who participate, we should look higher for our heroes. Our heroes—and our children's heroes—should be the saints. We should keep a good number of children's biographies of the saints easily accessible to our children. Some wonderful options include:

- *Miniature Stories of the Saints* by Fr. Daniel Lord

- The many saint stories written and illustrated by Tommie de Paola for little tots

- *Helen's Special Picture* by David Previtali, for early readers

- *The Man Who Never Died* and *The Man Who Dared a King* by Fr. Gerald Brennan

- *Marguerite* by Sr. St. Stephen (a reprint by Little Flower Family Apostolates)

- The *Saints and Friendly Beasts* series by Eva Betz (reprinted by Neumann Press)

- *Margaret* by Sr. M. Juliana (also reprinted by Neumann Press)

- *The Children's St. Anthony* and *The Children's St. Francis* by Catherine Beebe (recently reprinted by Refuge of Sinners Publishing and available at JoyfulCatholic.com)

- *Little Nellie* by Sr. Mary Dominic (reprinted by TAN)

- *The Orphans Find a Home* by Joan Stromberg

- *Dominic Savio* by Peter Lappin (reprinted by Roman Catholic Books).

- The coloring books by Mary Fabyan Windeatt, reprinted by TAN Books, which feature not only lovely illustrations but simple biographies of the saints for younger children

- *Saints of the Eucharist, Volumes I and II*, two coloring books by Fr. Francis, available from JoyfulCatholic.com

- *In the Footsteps of the Saints* series (now available from Emmanuel Books), although parents should read the books before giving them to their children, as some are rather gory or otherwise not appropriate for young children.

- Saint biographies written by Mary Fabyan Windeatt, reprinted by TAN Books, for children in fourth grade and up. These biographies beautifully integrate lessons on Catholic doctrine and spirituality into the text.

- The excellent <u>Vision Books</u>, many of which have been reprinted by Ignatius Press.

- *God's Heroes in America*, a comic book containing stories of nine American saints (available from JoyfulCatholic.com)

- <u>*Faces of Courage*</u> by the Daughters of St. Paul

- *Twenty-One Saints* by Aloysius Croft

- <u>*Treasure of the Mohawks*</u> and *The Fisherman's Ring* by Teri Martini

<u>These are</u> all excellent and inspiring books that youngsters will read over and over.

For high school students, there are many beautiful and inspiring biographies of saints, as well as other holy men and women, such as:

- *Lay Siege to Heaven* or *The Quiet Light* by Louis de Wohl

- *Blessed Margaret of Castello* by Fr. William R. Bonniwell

- *The Cure D'Ars* by Trochu

- <u>*The Shadow of His Wings*</u> by Fr. Gereon Goldmann

- *The Life of Father De Smet* by Fr. E. Laveille (which is superb but very long, so reluctant readers may prefer the shorter *Giant of the Western Trail* by Fr. Michael McHugh, reprinted by Neumann Press)

- *At the End of the Santa Fe Trail* by Sr. Blandina

- *Florence Nightingale's Nuns* by Emmeline Garnet

- *The Man Who Got Even with God* by Fr. Raymond

- *Fighting Father Duffy* by Virginia Lee Bishop and Jim Bishop (not currently in print)

- *Charity Goes to War* by Anne Heagney (not in currently print)

There are many more to choose from, as a visit to the local Catholic book store will reveal. Reading the stories of these heroic men and women will inspire our children to want to give their lives for God. (Many of these books provide the added benefit of incorporating historical events into the life of the holy person.)

Of course, if we have an opportunity to introduce our children to a priest, monk, or nun, we should take advantage of it so our children can get to know them and feel comfortable with them. Our parish priest should be spoken of with special respect, because he stands in the place of Christ and has the sacred power to hear confessions and celebrate Mass. If we have daughters, we can write to the

Council of Major Superiors of Women Religious in the United States of America for their free Vocations Directory which offers a photo and a description of many of the religious orders in this country. Our daughters may be intrigued to learn about the various apostolates of different religious orders, including those who live cloistered lives, those who teach children, those who nurse incurable cancer patients, those who care for the elderly, or those who serve as missionaries to other countries. There is even a religious order, the Sisters of Life, which is entirely devoted to a pro-life apostolate, including caring for women in crisis pregnancies. We can check out some of these religious orders online with our daughters. Some of the websites are fabulous, and we may want to print out some information about the spirituality of the order, the sisters' daily schedule, or the stories of how some of the postulants discerned their vocations. If our girls are interested in a religious order that doesn't have an informative website, we can at least find out the address and write to them for information. We can also look for religious orders of priests and monks for our sons or find information about the daily life of a diocesan priest.

If we foster a love of the sacraments and a strong spiritual life in our children and present them with models of the priesthood and religious life, often they will respond by dressing up as nuns or priests in their games, which shows that they consider a priestly or religious vocation as a viable, and admirable, option. There are books and toys specifically meant to spark this kind of play among children, such as the charming picture book, *The Adventures of Sister Regina Marie* by Zelie Redmond, "Holy Habits" paper dolls of nuns available from leafletonline.com, *The Right to Be Merry* for teenage girls, and videos on the priesthood and religious vocation for teens. Little boys often enjoy imitating their parish priest celebrating Mass with either homemade or store-bought Mass kits, such as the expensive but unbreakable toy Mass kit made by Wee Believers and sold by leafletonline.com, or the even more expensive but more realistic set sold bywayofthefamily.com. (Knowing how hard boys are on toys, we may find a homemade set more practical.)

Basically, the things we can do to encourage vocations among our children are the same things we would do just to help our children grow in holiness. Whether our children decide to enter the convent or the priesthood, live a single life, or marry, they need a strong spiritual life and a deep love of God to live their vocation in holiness so that they will become saints. This is our ultimate goal for our children, that they become saints. If we are forming our children to be saints, then our job is complete. God will call those whom He chooses, and they will be ready.

# 35

## OUTSIDE ACTIVITIES

*"The home is the schoolhouse for affection*
*wherein a mother completes the work that was*
*begun when the child was born."*
—ARCHBISHOP FULTON J. SHEEN

OUTSIDE activities can really enhance our homeschool; children benefit by learning new skills, exercising, socializing, and simply enjoying themselves. However, families today have a tendency to forget that too much of a good thing is no longer good. All too often, parents overschedule their children until the parents feel like they live in their cars and family meals become a forgotten ideal, with many unseen consequences detrimental to our family's well-being and to our children's development.

We must remember that signing up for too many activities outside the home or attending too many social events puts stress on the entire family. Too many outside activities can weaken family unity and disrupt normal family activities, such as attending Mass together, eating dinner together, playing games together, or just relaxing together and enjoying each other's company. They can even conflict with family traditions like Jesse Tree readings every night during Advent or singing Christmas carols every night during the Christmas season, or praying the rosary together daily anytime during the year.

Therefore, we must strive to choose outside activities prudently. We can try to find activities for multiple ages so more than one sibling can participate. This will greatly reduce our own driving time as well as the total time spent outside the house, thereby cutting down stress and minimizing the disruption of family activities. We can also choose activities that occur only once or twice a week instead of every day, and avoid commitments that fall during dinnertime or on Sundays. If appropriate, we can attend activities as a family; for example, we can have the whole family attend a sports event so that we'll still be spending time together. Not everyone has to pay close attention to the game—we can allow siblings to bring a book or stationery—but at least we'll be together to share a passing thought or to answer questions. Obviously, there are other important factors when choosing activities for our children; the needs and interests of each child, the price, and the location of each activity. Also, the size of our family may help us decide; the more children, the fewer commitments we'll want to make per child.

During the process of selecting outside activities, we must keep in mind that, fun as outside activities are, they are not necessary for the development of most children. Children learn what they need best from their own families, in their own homes. Anything more is superfluous. Unless a child has no siblings close in age, he gets most of the socialization he needs at home. Now, if we have several girls but only one boy, or several boys but only one girl, we may want to find a way for our child to play with others of his or her own sex (although sisters and brothers learning to play together is an important part of their social education, too). Nevertheless, outside activities, while beneficial, are not absolutely necessary, and too many of them can be positively harmful.

Of course, we should not sign up our children for activities to assuage our own feelings of guilt or inadequacy or to compete with other families. In particular, team sports that involve several practices a week can put an undue stress on the chauffeuring parents and really break up family time, while leading children to focus inordinate time and effort to master skills that they'll never use again once they finish school. It's wiser to find activities that require minimal time commitment, that promote general flexibility or strength, or that teach more practical skills, such as martial arts. Too much pressure to win is another pitfall of many sports. If we want our children to be good losers and gracious winners, then we'll choose activities that don't place too much emphasis on competition, but rather concentrate more on developing the children's skills.

All that we've said about outside activities also applies to social or educational events hosted by homeschooling groups or even families and friends. We can participate insofar as our family benefits and feels refreshed from the social interaction, and stop before we start feeling stressed or before we find ourselves with no time left to do basic housework. Pressure from friends or guilt trips from relatives must be dealt with firmly and not be allowed to influence our decisions for our family.

We should consider that not only does overscheduling outside activities disrupt family unity and time spent together, it can also threaten the spontaneous, imaginative play that children need for their formation and development. We must not make the mistake of thinking that a child's play is a meaningless activity solely for entertainment value. On the contrary, children process the information they learn and make it their own by playing. Play is also a preparation for adulthood, as children act out different roles, different careers, and different choices. Unstructured play with others helps children learn to communicate well with each other, to think creatively, to problem-solve, to compromise, to make and follow reasonable rules, and to work together. Playing alone allows the child to have some time of his own to process all that has been going on in his life and to relax in the one arena where he doesn't have to worry about doing things someone else's way and following other people's rules; he is king of all he surveys, at least for a few hours. Playing by himself allows a child time away from the stress he experiences from his interaction with others, and enables him to return, emotionally and psychologically refreshed. Unstructured play, both with others and by oneself, is necessary for a child's emotional and educational well-being.

If we still have lingering doubts about the value of unstructured play, we should consider an experiment described in *Einstein Never Used Flashcards* by Roberta Michnick Golinkoff, Kathy Hisrch-Pasek, and Diane Ever. During this experiment, three groups of children were told to sit on chairs where they could see a box with toys just out of reach. They were told that they could play with the toys, but they couldn't leave their seats to get the box. Instead, they were given rods, which could be attached together to make a long enough rod to reach the box and pull it over. The first group of children was allowed to play with the rods for several minutes before being told to use the rods to reach the box. The second group was not given time to play with the rods, but an adult showed them how to attach the rods together. The third group was given neither time to play with the rods nor a demonstration on how to attach the rods together. In the first group that was allowed to play with the rods before the experiment, all of the children were able to piece the rods together and pull the box over. In the second group, who had watched an adult piece the rods together, some of the children were able to follow the adult's example and reach the box, whereas others tried and gave up quickly when their first attempt failed. In the third group, which had neither time to play nor a demonstration, none of the children were able to put the rods together and reach the box of toys. What does this experiment tell us? Primarily, that children learn better through spontaneous, unstructured play than from an adult's instruction! We homeschoolers need to keep this in mind lest we rely too exclusively on activities devised and structured by adults.

In addition, by spending lots of time at home, instead of bustling off from one activity to another, our families will learn the age-old lesson that happiness comes from within ourselves, not from distractions from without. So many people in our society are afraid to spend time alone or to think. They are petrified of having nothing to do, unable to cope with boredom, and they have no idea how to entertain themselves without a television, a so-called "smart" phone, or a scheduled activity. Even their prayers are nothing but talking at God. They depend on a constantly active life to shield them from consideration of their own mortality and inadequacy, and they squelch their inner need for quiet meditation on transcendental truths and their yearning for a more profound relationship with God.

By spending lots of time at home, our children learn to overcome boredom, to entertain themselves, and to make quiet thought, and even meditation, a habit. They build the strength and confidence to deal with the demands made on them at home and outside. This is the quiet self-reliance and creativity that we want to encourage in our children— simply by keeping them at home and giving them time and space to grow.

Fortunately, most homeschooling families tend to spend more time at home, both on family activities and on the unstructured, spontaneous play that children need for their development. Still, even homeschooling families can be dazzled by the benefits of outside activities or social events and overschedule to the detriment of a peaceful, unhectic home life. Our home is our family's haven from this world; a place of peace and leisure where we bond with each other, where we spend time with the people who matter most to us, and where we build the energy and confidence to meet outside commitments. If we do not provide our family with the time to relax and refresh at home together, then we will not have the strength we need to deal with the outside world. Therefore, in choosing outside activities for our children, let us discuss our choices with the Lord and with our spouse, and then make our decision, remembering to be willing to pull out of any activity that puts undue strain on our family. Above all, let us provide our children with an abundance of unstructured time to play, think, build, draw, meditate, pray, and blossom.

# 36

## DELEGATION

*"All life demands a struggle. Those who
have everything given to them become lazy,
selfish, and insensitive to the real values
of life. The very striving and hard work that
we so constantly try to avoid is the major
building block in the person we are today."*

—POPE PAUL VI

DELEGATION is necessary for our sanity and for
the success of our homeschool. We cannot hope to
accomplish all we need to do if we do not recruit help from
our children.

That is not to say that delegation is always easy. When
children are young, it often takes more of our time to let
them help than otherwise, for we must show them how
to do each task, watch them do it, and sometimes redo it
when they leave the room. As they grow older, we must
train them to do work thoroughly—without nagging. We
must learn the balance of which imperfections to accept

versus what a strong work ethic demands, and how much praise a child needs for his efforts.

Some of us may feel guilty for requiring our children help us with housework or with the care of younger children. However, helping out with such work is not only *not* detrimental, but actually very beneficial to children, giving them a sense of accomplishment, confidence, self-esteem, and responsibility. They learn skills they'll need later in life, and they feel the satisfaction of contributing to the well-being of the family. They also learn self-sacrifice and develop the habit of watching out for those who are younger or weaker than themselves. Last, but surely not least, they have the benefit of living with a relaxed, happy mother who has more time to play games with them or read to them or just sit and chat with them.

We must remember, too, that public and parochial school children spend about seven hours a day in school, in addition to devoting a few more hours to homework every night. Since homeschooling consumes much less time, we need not feel guilty about giving our children a few chores around the house—in fact, if we did not, our children would most likely become quite spoiled and selfish.

In addition to helping them learn responsibility, chores can teach spiritual lessons, too. Our children must be taught that everything we do can be transformed into an act of love for God. From lessons to housework to watching the baby, we can offer every act to God and perform it out of love. We must teach our children to offer their day to God in their morning prayers, and then, throughout the day, renew this offering, particularly when they have something unpleasant to do. This makes labor sweeter, for it gives our chores new meaning. Any romantic youngster will admit that a man toiling to win the hand of his fair lady experiences some real satisfaction in his labors because he is doing it out of love; so, also, our own work and our own suffering takes on a new sweetness when we lift our hearts to God and embrace our work or our pain out of love for him. Did not Our Lord tell us, "Come to me, all you that labor and are burdened: I will refresh you. Take up my yoke upon you and learn of me, because I am meek and humble of heart: and you shall find rest to your souls. For my yoke is sweet and my burden light" (Matthew 11:28-30)?

Let us tell our children of how St. Therese of Lisieux, unable to offer any heroic deeds or martyrdom to Our Lord, offered Him the daily annoyances of having dirty water splashed in her face as she washed her clothes, or her trepidation in cleaning a cabinet that might harbor spiders. By offering these petty trials to God, she changed her annoying chores into acts of love and transformed herself into a saint.

Every household has its own system and ways, and children mature at different rates; however, here are some suggestions for chores, as long as we keep in mind that some children might be ready for the following chores at different ages than those suggested:

- children old enough to sleep in a bed are old enough to make their bed

- children out of diapers can mostly dress themselves

- children age five and up can set the table or help clear the table

- children of five and up can match socks

- children six or seven and up can wash most of the dishes, except for some of the hard-to-scrub pots

- children of nine or ten can put the laundry in the washer and dryer, and can fold clothes and put them away

- children of all different ages can do increasingly difficult tasks in the kitchen, including greasing a pan, cracking and beating an egg, measuring flour, mixing batter, opening a can, de-chunking tuna fish, making sandwiches, etc.

- With our supervision, teens can learn to chop vegetables, stir a sauce or boil pasta on the stove, or flip pancakes

- children old enough to read can read to younger siblings

- children eight and up could be employed to teach the younger ones to tie their shoes or to keep an eye on the toddlers while we make dinner or take a shower

- shoveling snow, raking leaves, mowing the grass, vacuuming, dusting, and other jobs can be assigned according to our children's maturity

Of course, children need plenty of free time for spontaneous, imaginative play of all kinds, for developing hobbies, and for reading. We do not want to burden our children beyond their years. However, prudent delegation of household chores can not only contribute to our own peace of mind, but also to the formation of responsible, competent, confident, and unselfish children. Let us not neglect this inestimable resource that the good Lord has given us!

# 37

## FATHERS

*"Christian husband! Imitate St. Joseph by
beginning your day's work with God, and
ending it for Him. Cherish those belonging to
you as the holy foster father did Jesus, and be
their faithful protector."*

—ST. JOHN VIANNEY

WHAT is a father's role in a homeschool? The
father's role varies from one homeschooling family
to another.

In rare situations, the father stays home and teaches the
children himself. This could be because his wife is ill or has
died, or because he's been laid off and his wife has taken
a job to help out financially until he finds work again.
Whatever the reason, this is a challenging situation because
many fathers feel self-conscious about staying home with
their children, and they also may have trouble finding other
stay-at-home homeschooling fathers to hang out with. In
a troubled economy, however, this situation occurs more
frequently, and a man must realize that he is fulfilling his

manly duty as a husband and father in choosing the path that is best for his family, even though it is difficult and not always understood by others. Furthermore, though nurturing and teaching young children does not come naturally to many men, fathers should remember that they have their own gifts and interests that will bring a new richness to their children's education. Fathers can share their sense of adventure, creativity, problem-solving skills, and humor with their children, all of which will add unique spice to a homeschool. Lastly, a father who gives his time, energy, and love to his children by homeschooling them each day can only grow wiser, holier, and more loving by accepting this difficult, but rewarding, challenge.

Nevertheless, in most homeschooling families, the mother stays home and teaches the children, and she may wonder what her husband's role ought to be. Ideally, the answer would be that the husband's role is to do whatever his wife needs him to do. Juggling housework, meals, and the children's education is not easy, especially if we still have a baby or a toddler to care for. Husbands may remember their own mothers as self-sufficient in housework and cooking and think that their wives don't need any more help than their mothers did. Since most of us were not homeschooled, however, the comparison does not really hold. A homeschooling mother cannot get nearly as much housework done during the day because she is busy with lessons and supervising the children even when lessons are over. Furthermore, husbands who think their mothers got no help with housework or cooking are probably not remembering accurately the years when their mothers were pregnant or just had a baby or had many little ones but no children big enough to really contribute substantial assistance. All mothers need help during these times, and homeschooling mothers need even more.

As homeschooling mothers, we should spend each week getting everything done that we can—and what we can't get to, our husband can help with on the weekend, or whenever he has time off. This may not mean teaching our children a subject or two, although some husbands do. Maybe our husband can spend part of his free time finishing whatever household chores we couldn't get to. Or he can watch the children while we get out by ourselves for a couple hours each week; take all the children out once a week so we can get some housework done without interruptions; occasionally make dinner, help clean, or run errands for us on his way home from work; or even buy a pizza or some other quick meal, without complaining when we didn't have the time to get dinner on the table. Sometimes all we need is for our husband to listen to our concerns and worries, giving thoughtful advice when we are perplexed and providing loving encouragement when we feel discouraged. It may mean our husband will call home every day to see how our day is going and to give us a little pep talk when we need it—or just a chance to talk to another adult for a few minutes. If we are struggling with maintaining discipline, perhaps our husband can support us by calling home and speaking to the rebellious child over the phone during the day. Perhaps he can look over the children's work every week to impress the children with the importance of their lessons.

Ironically, knowing that our husband will do whatever chores we can't get to during the week may help motivate us to get more done because our normal, dull chores have been transformed more visibly into acts of love. Whatever we get done during the week our husband doesn't have to do on the weekend. This knowledge can give us the impetus to accomplish more, without the nagging pressure that if we don't do it, it won't get done.

For a family to homeschool successfully, both parents need to work together to fill each other's needs and to support each other. Demanding that our husband help us in these ways is not, of course, the best approach. However, our husband may not know what we need if we don't talk to him. Most loving and reasonable husbands will pitch in if they realize their help is needed, especially if a happier, less stressed wife is their reward. The key is teamwork, working together, not blaming each other for past failures, but asking humbly for the future. It involves explaining our needs and seeking a solution together. We must lay aside selfishness and laziness and be willing to do what seems like more than our share of the work because often we don't realize how much effort our spouse is actually putting forth. Of course, a husband who works overtime or whose job is mentally or physically draining may not be able to help as much as a husband who works regular hours and finds his job deeply fulfilling. However, we can't assume that because our husband works long hours, he cannot help us. If we discuss our needs openly with him, we may be surprised at the solutions he comes up with. He may think up ways we can delegate some of the jobs to the children or reorganize our schedule or our space for greater productivity, for example.

When our husband does help out, we must try to remember to show our appreciation. We should thank him, even if the task he does is small or is part of his usual list of chores. After all, we enjoy being thanked for making dinner even though it is one of our regular jobs. But even more than verbal thanks, we should show our appreciation by acting more cheerful and relaxed. All too often, the tendency is to focus on something that needs to be done, and as soon as it's done, to find some other job to focus on. Granted, we're living in a fallen world where new problems crop up frequently, we should still try to keep our expectations reasonable, and make a habit of focusing on the chores that have been completed, expressing our appreciation in both words and attitude.

Different couples have different needs and different systems for dividing the work. What's most important is that we lovingly communicate our own needs, respect our spouse's needs, and work together to accomplish what must be done. Taking the Holy Family as our model, we can strive to imitate the patience, gentleness, and cheerfulness of Our Lady, and ask St. Joseph to help our husband to imitate his manly self-sacrifice, his piety, and his kindness.

# 38

## NATURAL HOME REMEDIES

*"With the earth was the human being created.*
*All the elements served mankind and, sensing*
*that man was alive, they busied themselves in*
*aiding his life in every way."*

—ST. HILDEGARDE DE BINGEN

THE connection between using natural home remedies and homeschooling may not be immediately apparent, but many homeschooling parents who have taken charge of their family's education benefit greatly by also taking charge of their family's health. The first and most obvious benefit is that natural remedies such as herbs, homeopathic remedies, and essential oils are usually less expensive than conventional, allopathic medicine. This is a great boon to a family economizing because one parent must stay home to educate the children. Secondly, if we become knowledgeable about natural treatment for common, everyday ailments, then we can save both time and money by avoiding unnecessary doctor visits, which, again, can make our homeschooling days run more smoothly.

Thirdly, natural remedies can benefit us because natural remedies address the underlying cause and speed healing, whereas allopathic medicine tends to treat the symptoms, not the cause, sometimes even leaving the patient worse off than he was before.

Let's look at a couple of examples. When dealing with a typical flu or cold, allopathic medicine involves lowering the fever, suppressing the cough, and drying up the runny nose. Yet the fever, cough, and runny nose are the body's ways of fighting the disease. By counteracting the body's natural responses to disease, allopathic medicines actually slow down recovery. On the other hand, natural remedies, such as eucalyptus oil (diluted in olive oil and rubbed on the chest and neck), raw honey, ginger, mullein, slippery elm, elderberry, and echinacea, work with the body in promoting healing by breaking up congestion, making dry coughs more productive, soothing the sore throat while fighting infection, and supporting the body's immune system. Naturopathy generally does not involve lowering a fever, except sometimes at night so parents and child can get some much needed rest; if a medicine like Tylenol is used, naturopathy would also administer milk thistle to counter its harmful side effects on the liver. Another example would be ear infections. Most doctors still prescribe antibiotics for ear infections, even though antibiotics kill both good and bad bacteria, paving the way for recurring ear infections and, for many children, the insertion of ear tubes, an invasive and unpleasant procedure. Natural remedies for ear infections, however, involve applying garlic-mullein drops to ease the pain and fight infection, while taking immunity-boosting herbs, such as echinacea, orally. Persistent or outer ear infections may respond better to goldenseal drops in the ear. These herbs eliminate the ear infection without killing the good bacteria, thereby greatly reducing the chances of the child coming down with another infection. Best of all, most herbs and other natural remedies do not bring the risk of dangerous or unpleasant side effects, although we do need to be aware of any contraindications, as not all herbs are safe for everyone.

Because herbs and other natural remedies can affect our bodies powerfully, we must research to make sure the remedies we use are safe. For example, raw honey soothes a sore throat and fights infection, but is not safe to administer to a child under eighteen months. Likewise, feverfew has helped many people avoid migraine headaches, but it is not safe to take during pregnancy or breastfeeding, while licorice, an herb sometimes used for sore throats and coughs, is not safe for people with high blood pressure. Moreover, there are situations that cannot be dealt with safely at home, for example, when meningitis is suspected or when a child allergic to bee venom gets stung.

If we choose to employ home remedies, then we must find reliable sources, such as *Naturally Healthy Babies and Children* by Aviva Jill Romm. This book is particularly helpful for homeschooling families because Mrs. Romm includes safe dosages and treatments for infants and children, which most naturopathic books do not do. Aviva Jill Romm has also written *The Natural Pregnancy Book* and *Vaccinations: A Thoughtful Parents' Guide*, which may be useful. (Her book on pregnancy does sometimes reveal a slight New Age slant, and some of the pictures are inappropriate for children, but we can ignore the New Age references, black out the pictures, and benefit from her suggestions for safe remedies for many common ailments during pregnancy.) Another excellent source of information on naturopathy for adults is *The Healing Power of Vitamins, Minerals, and Herbs*, put out by Reader's Digest. We may want to look for good books on essential oils or homeopathy, as well, or at least find some informative, reliable websites to assist us in caring for the medical needs of our family.

Another reason homeschooling families often like using natural remedies is that they have learned through homeschooling that the "experts" don't have all the answers. Homeschooling parents learn not to be intimidated by educators who throw around a lot of "teacherese" jargon about skills and concepts to be learned at each grade level. In the same way, more homeschoolers are learning that the doctors who try to scare us with medical catastrophes that will ensue if we do not submit to their prescriptions, vaccines, and invasive procedures, are not the infallible guides we thought them to be. Since we will reap the good or bad results of how we educate and medicate ourselves, shouldn't we research these areas and take charge ourselves?

Lastly, homeschooling works well with using natural remedies because it's educational! As we immerse ourselves in books on herbs and natural healing and begin to frequent stores selling herbs and homeopathic remedies, our children's interest will be piqued. When they see us treating them with various herbs or natural salves, they'll ask us questions. They'll learn about how the body works, how herbs help the body heal itself, and what herbs to use under different circumstances. They will also see how a healthy diet and exercise play a crucial role in good health. Natural healing will become a part of their lives, and they will be prepared to take charge of their own health as they grow up. Perhaps most importantly, they'll learn not to passively accept the opinion of the "experts," but to question, research, and take responsibility for whatever situation comes up in their lives.

# 39

## GRANDPARENTS

*"I am speaking of [my grandmother] the illustrious Macrina, by whom we were taught the words of the blessed Gregory [Thaumaturgos], which, having preserved until her time by uninterrupted tradition, she also guarded, and she formed and molded me, still a child, in doctrines of piety."*

—ST. BASIL THE GREAT

OUR children's grandparents are naturally concerned about our children receiving the best education. Depending on what they've heard about homeschooling, they may not be very supportive of our choice to educate our children at home. Fortunately, homeschooling has become more mainstream in recent years, and negative attitudes about it are less common, especially as the poor performance of the public schools becomes so well publicized. Nevertheless, not everyone views homeschooling as a positive thing, and our parents or in-laws may be among those who don't.

When dealing with family members critical of homeschooling, we can try to present them with the facts about homeschooling. In 2009, the National Home Education Research Institute released a study that showed homeschoolers who use a wide range of learning styles outperformed students from conventional schools on standardized tests, regardless of the parents' own level of education or income bracket. We can also point out the multitude of problems with the school system today. The academic standards have been dumbed down because of the amount of time most students spend in passive activities, like watching television, has stunted their intellectual growth. Moreover, the degrading, crude TV programs, movies, and music that most children are immersed in and the immodest styles of clothing make school culture most objectionable. And although people used to question homeschoolers' socialization, the kinds of unhealthy socialization that occurs in schools—such as bullying, ridicule, and peer pressure—have convinced many parents to remove their children from schools.

Of course, we haven't even mentioned the politically correct or otherwise inappropriate content of the actual curricula being taught in most schools. We can find some informative articles or books on the advantages of homeschooling if our relatives are interested enough to read them, particularly if they are concerned about the effects of homeschooling a disabled child, for example. Some grandparents may feel that our decision to homeschool is somehow a criticism of their decision to send their own children to public or private school. We can truthfully assure them (even if we wish we had been homeschooled because we are so familiar now with the benefits) that their situation was entirely different from our own; schools are much worse now than they were even one generation ago, and homeschooling was unheard of in many parts of the country. We can try our best to applaud the efforts they took in raising their children and point out how society and education have changed since then.

Many grandparents, upon learning the benefits of homeschooling and the sad condition of today's schools, will quickly change their attitude and encourage us to homeschool. Others will not. If our parents or in-laws continue to question or criticize our decision after we have respectfully explained our reasons, then we must take a firm line, requesting that they respect the decision we've made and not keep bringing it up. This is extremely important. Confidence is a huge issue for homeschoolers; we need to do whatever we can to bolster our own confidence and courage in the choice we have made. If our relatives continue to heap negativity upon us, we may need to limit our interaction with them, at least temporarily. Hopefully, when our parents or in-laws see that our children are well-spoken, well-informed, curious, lively, and comfortable with socializing with different age groups, they will begin to change their minds and support our decision.

Sometimes older people like to test homeschooled children by constantly quizzing them on things they think children in a particular grade should know. If our children don't mind and know the answers at least most of the time, this may not pose a problem. However, many children will not appreciate pop quizzes whenever they visit their grandparents, and their relationship with their grandparents may suffer. Moreover, if our relatives do this as a way of testing our choice to homeschool, this will probably cause tension for us and for our children. If their quizzing our children makes us or our children uncomfortable for any reason, we must ask them kindly but firmly to stop, explaining that this makes us uncomfortable and impedes the nurturing, loving relationship children should have with their grandparents.

Obviously, we must use common sense when dealing with relatives hostile to homeschooling. If we have doubts about a child's progress or about our own capabilities, we need to confide these doubts to someone else, and share only positive stories with critical relatives.

Whether our children's grandparents approve of or oppose our decision to homeschool, we can try to allow them to get involved if they wish, as long as they keep their disapproval to themselves. Because homeschooling takes less time than conventional school, we may be able to visit grandparents during the day and provide them the opportunity of spending special time with their grandchildren. Grandparents may enjoy listening to a young child reading aloud or helping an older child with a craft or science project. Grandparents may also be interested in teaching our children to knit, bake, garden, whittle, golf, or to share whatever interests they have. Our children can interview them for history or geography class, asking them about wars, recessions, or other historical events they have lived through, or asking them about different states or countries they have visited. Children who have not been raised on a steady diet of TV and computers are more open to the sometimes slow-paced conversation of older people. At the same time, grandparents will often appreciate children who make eye contact and take the time to chat without multiple interruptions to text someone else. If we wonder where we will keep all the projects or crafts that our children create, sometimes these can be given as gifts to grandparents who will cherish these creative treasures.

If our children's grandparents live far away, we can try to send lots of photos of the children and their projects. We can also develop our children's writing skills by having them write letters to their grandparents frequently. Most likely, these letters will be treasured by grandparents who recall a time when a long-distance telephone call was a big event, emailing was unknown, and letter-writing was an art.

Grandparents can truly be a blessing for our family in our educational journey. We and our children can learn from their wisdom and their unique perspectives, and we can sit back and enjoy watching our grandparents and our children interact. Let us pray to St. Anne and St. Joachim, the grandparents of Christ, to ease whatever friction exists in our relationships and to help both our families and our relatives to benefit from our time spent together.

# 40

## STRUGGLES IN HOMESCHOOLING

*"Jesus is the teacher of holiness. I go to Him*
*because I want Him to teach me how to*
*become a Saint. Of what use to me is all I*
*learn in school if I do not become holy?"*

—ST. FRANCIS DE SALES, AS A BOY

ALTHOUGH homeschooling is usually a natural and joyful way of life, we all struggle sometimes. The stain of original sin is removed at baptism, but our intellects remain darkened and our wills weakened, and we are prey to our own concupiscence. Sometimes our temperaments clash with the temperaments of our children; sometimes a child goes through a rebellious or disrespectful stage; sometimes a child's perfectionism brings on tears at the slightest mistake until every lesson becomes a weeping session; sometimes we find ourselves unable to effectively teach a concept to a child for reasons unknown.

Identifying the problem that confronts us is half the battle. Do our child's difficulties during lessons stem from a lack of interest, from laziness, or from a difference in learning style? Is the book we're using dull or hard to understand? Is the child so emotionally troubled about something that he can't focus on his lessons? Is he getting enough sleep at night? Discovering what the problem is can be difficult. Prayer, reflection, and discussion with our spouse and with the child can lead us to an accurate assessment of the situation. But no matter what the cause of the trouble, disrespect or disobedience from a child must not be tolerated. We have to maintain discipline and respect. In the meantime, we can try to discover if there is a reason behind the disrespectful behavior; perhaps the child is stressed or angry over a friend moving away, or the ridicule of some neighborhood children, or a family issue. Perhaps he doesn't understand our decision to remove him from school and homeschool him. We can gently encourage our children to talk to us about whatever is bothering them, validating their wounded feelings with sympathy and offering a spiritual perspective on the situation.

Once we think we've identified the problem, we can start trying solutions. Of course, sometimes we have to use the old trial and error method before we know for sure if we've pinpointed the problem correctly. If a child is struggling with his lessons, we can try to make lessons more interesting, letting him have some choice in the books we use, or making the material easier by going more slowly. A perfectionist or scrupulous child may benefit from educational games rather than a sheet of questions or problems where he has to worry about how many he'll get wrong.

Other children feel confused by worksheets but can readily explain what they have learned orally or on paper. Or we may realize that the problem is as simple as not getting enough sleep and change the child's bedtime. (Sometimes if a child goes to bed too early, he lies awake so long that he can't fall asleep even when he normally would, so too early a bedtime can be just as problematic as too late.) If there is a particular concept that the child is struggling with, we can try a different approach—sometimes examples from real life help the information to click in a child's mind. But if we try several different approaches, and nothing seems to work, we might decide the child simply isn't ready yet for the material we're trying to teach. Perhaps the child has sensed our stress and frustration and feels so tense when the subject is introduced that he can't focus properly. Or possibly the child is just not mentally ready for this concept yet. Education isn't a one-age-fits-all process; different children are ready for new skills at different ages. Often putting the material aside for just a few months, sometimes longer, will do the trick. Then we can try to reintroduce the topic in a relaxed, even playful, way that won't cause the child renewed anxiety.

Sometimes we can benefit by discovering each child's learning style. To begin with, some children are visual learners. They may have trouble listening to lectures or read-alouds; they may prefer to read along silently or write down what is being read or talked about. For the most part, they will enjoy reading by themselves and will benefit from diagrams or drawings.

Auditory learners, on the other hand, benefit more from listening than from reading. They'll enjoy having us read aloud to them and listening to books on tape. They may also like to learn math facts or state capitals by listening to the "You Never Forget What You Sing" CDs sold by bywayofthefamily.com, or by making up their own songs or poems about what they're learning.

Kinesthetic learners learn best with hands-on activities, especially using objects with interesting textures. Many children with ADHD will be kinesthetic learners. Cuisenaire rods, an abacus, plastic globes, plastic models of the body, simple crafts or science experiments, and other hands-on tools will help them make the most of their lessons. Expensive equipment is not necessary. Tracing letters in shaving cream, counting Cheerios to learn to learn addition or probability, doing simple experiments using household items—these are the kinds of activities that will help a kinesthetic learner become excited about lessons. If we don't have the time or energy to come up with activities for every subject, we can rely on some of the books crammed full of ideas for hands-on lessons. As soon as our child is old enough to read and work independently, we can give them such a book and tell them to choose one activity each day, or each week, and only ask for help as needed. Most children will learn better if they are able to choose and direct their own activities, while the book will ensure the activities are related to their lessons. Many children's books on science offer a wide variety of science experiments, including Janice VanCleave's popular series, and there are even history craft books, some of which are listed in our chapter on history.

While trying to discern the cause of our struggle in homeschooling a particular child, we may come to suspect that our child has a learning disability. Challenging though learning disabilities can be, once we have diagnosed the problem, we can research what strategies work best for children with this particular problem, and our lessons should quickly grow less frustrating and more productive. The more we can find out about our child's learning disability, the better we can help him overcome the obstacles that face him. We can thank Our Lord from our hearts that we have the opportunity to homeschool our child, as most children with learning disabilities thrive in a one-on-one learning environment where their particular needs are met and there are fewer distractions.

Whatever our situation, we may at times find ourselves growing discouraged or doubting our own ability to homeschool during these struggles. But we must trust in God to enlighten us and strengthen us. He has given us each child; He will surely give us the resources we need to care for and educate them. We may feel inadequate or guilty for removing our children from school, but we must assure ourselves that our children would not learn any better from an expert at a conventional school. While the teacher at school may be an expert in learning disabilities, only we are experts about our own children. We love them more than anyone else, we know them better than anyone else, we are more willing to be flexible and try different teaching techniques than anyone else, and we are more capable of providing a warm, nurturing, positive, and holy environment for our child than anyone else could be.

We must also remember through these challenging times that our child can sense our anxiety and frustration and will internalize these emotions, dimly aware that somehow he is the cause of them. Therefore, our trust in God, and the calm serenity which follows, is vital not only for our well-being, but for our child's as well. We must try to keep everything in perspective and ask ourselves, "What do I want my child to learn from his lesson today?" Yes, we want him to learn the material we are covering, but what else? Having our child learn when to use a comma or how to multiply fractions may be our immediate goal, but it will not help him achieve the only really important goal in life: getting to heaven. Watching his mother teach him patiently day in and day out, correct him gently, and laugh with him over mistakes—this will give him a glimpse of God's love for him, and that *will* help him get to heaven.

Academic goals are important, but let's not allow them to overshadow our ultimate goal: to raise our children to be saints. And we can accomplish this best simply by loving them.

# 41

# HOMESCHOOLING CHILDREN WITH ATTENTION DEFICIT/HYPERACTIVITY DISORDER

*"Instead of sleeping peacefully in his crib, Baby spent his time contemplating ways to dismantle it, and we think he may have set some sort of record. At six weeks he had jammed the slide side; at three months he had bashed in the back panel; and we have yet to figure out how old he was when he crawled out of the crib and removed the castors."*

—TERESA BLOOMINGDALE,
COLUMNIST, AUTHOR AND
MOTHER OF TEN

PARENTS of children who are hyperactive and have short attention spans can be very grateful for the opportunity to homeschool. Although dealing with hyperactive children all day can exhaust and exasperate us at times,

273

we will have the satisfaction of knowing our children will thrive at home in an environment that respects their individuality, provides an outlet for their energy, incorporates their learning style into the lessons, and above all avoids a school system that would destroy their self-esteem with labels or medicate them into compliant, conforming, robots. Moreover, as we watch our children succeed in the environment we are striving to create for them, chances are we will slowly find our children less exhausting, less exasperating, and more fun to be with.

Homeschooling is a wonderful option for children who have been diagnosed with Attention Deficit Hyperactivity Disorder (ADHD—or who might have been diagnosed with ADHD, had they attended a conventional school. Children who have been diagnosed with ADHD exhibit a wide range of symptoms, due to the subjectivity of the diagnostic process, but even severe cases do not necessarily need to be treated with medication, and the flexibility of homeschooling allows us to try a wider variety of natural treatments. First of all, children diagnosed with ADHD tend perform poorly in a classroom setting but thrive when taught one-on-one, which is exactly what happens with homeschooling. Furthermore, the attention span of hyperactive children often lasts much longer when their lessons incorporate their natural interests. Unit studies or even unschooling might work well. We can experiment to see what method engages their interest. Their attention spans might expand surprisingly when their curiosity is aroused.

Obviously, hyperactive children will find it difficult to sit down for a long time to do lessons. Again, because homeschooling requires only a fraction of the time that conventional school takes, homeschooling can be a real sanity-saver for a bouncy, restless child. Moreover, home-schoolers have the ability to allow children to take a quick break and run around the house or do fifty jumping jacks to get rid of some excess energy. We can even allow our children to move around while they learn—which may be best for kinesthetic learners anyway. Perhaps they could bounce a ball in rhythm as they recite their math facts, or write numbers on the ground with sidewalk chalk and jump on the correct answer as we call out math facts. In good weather, sidewalk chalk can take the place of pencils and paper; in cold or damp weather, we can make some kind of floor mat to use indoors, perhaps out of an old bedboard or a large, sturdy piece of cardboard. It may take a little imagination and time on our part to come up with active educational activities, but the results will be worth the effort. Rather than writing down answers to questions, kinesthetic learners or active children may like to draw dia-grams of what they're learning or keep a time-line or make models with clay or playdough or cardboard. (Old cereal boxes can be a great, though often overlooked, source of cardboard.) Answering questions orally will also be a good option, rather than having a restless child spend hours sit-ting down and writing answers. Some children may prefer to immerse themselves in one educational project for a few weeks, rather than doing a little of each subject every day;

instead of worrying about what our child is not learning, we should relish the fact that our child is enthusiastic about learning and encourage him as much as we can. Whatever subject he chooses, most likely he will eventually realize that he needs math skills, writing skills, and research skills to further pursue his interest. Thus many a unit study has been born. Many children with ADHD will be kinesthetic learners, so we can go over the suggestions in the previous chapter for helping kinesthetic learners.

Aside from trying different teaching techniques, there are other natural ways of helping a hyperactive child. Prayer, of course, should be our first recourse. Our child's guardian angel can assist us in choosing the most helpful resources for our child's situation. Our own guardian angel can help us to be patient and understanding with our sometimes exasperating offspring. We should also consult some helpful resources for educating hyperactive children, such as Aviva Jill Romm's *Naturally Healthy Babies and Children*. The book offers many different ideas for parents of hyperactive children, including:

- Enrolling them in a martial arts class, which will teach them discipline and provide a healthy outlet for their energy;

- Using natural herbs which may nourish their nervous system, promote calmness, and stabilize blood sugar;

- Eliminating refined sugar and food additives, such as preservatives and dyes, from their diets, particularly breakfast. (Although it requires great effort, the Feingold Diet has brought tremendous help to many families. For information and support, call the Feingold Association at 703-768-FAUS.)

• Providing more opportunities for exercise, especially outdoors, such as hiking;

• Considering whether there have been any traumatic events which may have upset our child, such as family illness or death, family arguments, or an unhappy experience at a school involving a lack of respect for his learning style or excessive ridicule from other students.

Aviva Jill Romm also recommends Dr. Thomas Armstrong's *The Myth of the ADD Child*, which offers many more tips that parents may find invaluable.

ADHD is a very controversial topic. Most people acknowledge it has been overly diagnosed, and some question whether it really should be listed as a disease subject to medical treatment at all. (It was not listed in the *Diagnostic and Statistical Manual of Mental Disorders* by the American Psychiatric Association until 1980.) Some teachers, overwhelmed by large classes of unruly students, find it easier to pressure parents to medicate their children than attempt the nearly impossible task of individualizing their teaching style for each child in their class. Often schools promote over-diagnosis because they receive more money from the government for each student diagnosed with a disability. Unfortunately, simply being labeled as ADHD can do incalculable harm to the child, damaging his self-esteem and giving him a built-in excuse to blame all his faults on, rather than working to correct them. Prescribing medicines for ADHD may harm the child even more, robbing him of his unique creativity, his zest for life, and the habit of overcoming his problems himself, as well as potentially leading to addiction and a host of other side effects that may last through adulthood.

Fortunately, homeschoolers are blessed with the flexibility to use one-on-one lessons, as well as experimenting with different learning styles, diets, herbs, and other natural means to bring out the best in our children, and to experience the thrill of watching our children respond and thrive in an environment that truly respects and fosters their unique gifts and personalities.

# 42

## WINTER BLUES

*"It is always springtime in a heart
that loves God."*

—ST. JOHN VIANNEY

THERE are times during the school year when, no matter how engaging our curriculum is, we experience a restlessness, a boredom, and a yearning for spring. Usually this occurs during the drab winter months of January, February, and March. The excitement of Christmas is over, the small penances of Lent aggravate us, the inclement weather prevents outdoor play except for an infrequent snowstorm, and winter seems to drag out longer than ever. How can charity and patience survive when a homeschooling family is pent up together in one house all day long, week after week? How can we escape burnout when battling frayed tempers, cabin fever, and an occasional flu?

One way to enliven the dreary winter months is to celebrate St. Valentine's Day and St. Patrick's Day with gusto. We can spend a few afternoons decorating the house and making ornate valentines for each member of the family, as well as grandparents or elderly neighbors. Red paper, stickers, glue, doilies, and scissors aren't expensive and can yield impressive results. Even old magazines or catalogs can add to the fun when children cut out pictures to decorate their masterpieces. To add to the excitement, we can plan a St. Valentine's Day show, possibly with a skit on the life of St. Valentine. Not much is known about his life, but we can research legends about him online or use Robert Saguda's picture book, *St. Valentine*, which tells a lovely legend about his life that could easily be turned into a short play.

We can celebrate St. Patrick's Day with similar festivities, decorating the house with shamrocks, Irish flags and leprechauns. There is an abundance of books about St. Patrick to form the basis of a short or long play, including Tomie DePaola's picture book, *Patrick: Patron Saint of Ireland*, or an easy reader like *The Story of St. Patrick* by James A. Janda, or the excellent Landmark book *The Life of St. Patrick* by Quentin Reynolds. We can find a CD with Irish songs, learn them together, and enjoy some singalongs, or each child could learn one song to perform for the rest of the family, ending with a reading of St. Patrick's famous prayer, "St. Patrick's Breastplate."

If we find other times of the year tedious or tiresome, we can look for other feast days to celebrate. We could celebrate the feast days of our children's patron saints, or the patron saint of schools, St. Thomas Aquinas (whose feast falls at the end of January, another bleak winter month), or any saint to whom our family has a devotion. Just look at the liturgical calendar and pick a saint we like, or perhaps a saint we'd like our family to get to know better, for that month. Depending on the age of our children, we or the children can read a short account of the life of the saint and write and direct a skit about it. Rather than depict the saint's entire life, perhaps we can dramatize one or two particular incidents in the saint's life, revealing a particular virtue. For example, young children could have fun playing Thomas Aquinas' brothers kidnapping young Thomas to prevent him from entering the Dominican Order; older children might be inspired while acting out the scene where the crucified Christ appears to Thomas and, praising him for all his theological writing, asks what he would like as a reward, to which Thomas responds, "Only You, Lord!" Alternately, we could find some quotes by the saint that our children can understand, and we can have them memorize and recite them, or we could have each child write a poem about the saint's life and read it aloud in front of the family. Of course, our celebration does not need to be limited to activities about the saint in question. We can add other entertaining and educational activities to liven up our school year, such as a sing-along, a family game, or some kind of informal family performance.

Performing in front of the family is a fun, but also very beneficial, form of recreation, with endless variations. Our children could each memorize one poem and recite it for the family. We can occasionally have themes to our poetry days, with each child could memorizing a limerick one week, and the next week each child learning a poem about an animal. Perhaps the recitation could end with all the children singing "Talk to the Animals." This would also be a good opportunity for children to perform a song on a musical instrument if they're taking lessons, or we could take this opportunity to teach them to sing in harmony. If we can't sing in harmony, we could teach our children a round, such as "Three Blind Mice," or we could teach our children to sing with synchronized hand movements or dance steps. Even boys benefit from the coordination and discipline required in learning to dance; moreover, if they ever do need to know how to dance, they'll be glad they already know instead of enduring the embarrassment of learning in order to dance with a particular girl. However, we must be sure never to offend our boys by requiring them to do effeminate steps, and we should remember to emphasize that to be a good dancer, a man must learn how to lead his partner with confidence, which symbolizes his eventual role as head of the family. Another possibility is having have each child do a short oral presentation on something they've learned in the past few weeks, like a country they've learned about, a science experiment they've done, a new math skill they've just mastered, or a person they've been reading about in history. The chance to use a small blackboard can be a great incentive for children to get up and explain what they've been learning. Two or more children could even act out a historical event or a scene from a classic they've recently read. The more poetic children might enjoy writing and reciting a poem about what they've learned in science or history, and the more musical might enjoy coming up with a song about what they're studying. Artistic children will want to enhance their presentation with a poster or paper maché model of their subject. Children can be amazingly creative when motivated. Furthermore, by getting up and performing in front of their own family, children learn to perform with poise and comfort in an informal setting without the stress or potential trauma of a public audience. They also need to master the material they've learned more completely in order to present it to others. Once the performance is over, we can end with a prayer written to or by the saint whose feast day it is.

Of course, any celebration seems more festive if it involves some kind of special food. Even in Lent, if we've given up sweets, or if we are trying to avoid sugar for health reasons, we can try to think of some food that isn't sweet and yet is different and a little festive, such as soft pretzels, popcorn fresh and hot from the stovetop, or scones. (Homemade is always best, but, if we're too stressed or busy, there is nothing wrong with supporting our local baker!)

Besides family performances, we can make the winter months more fun by incorporating more educational games in our curriculum. If we don't have the money to buy fancy board games, we can easily make our own, and our children will learn even more if they help. Math is often the most tedious subject during the long winter months, but it is also the easiest one to design games for. For other subjects, we could have our children make crossword puzzles for each other on what they're learning, especially if two are studying the same thing. Maybe this would be a good time to focus on science experiments or some other hands-on activities that will attract our children's attention. Whatever style of homeschooling we've chosen, we may want to introduce some kind of change to refresh and rekindle our family's interest. We could pick one or two days a week, for instance, Wednesdays and Fridays, to devote to educational games only, or to spend on science experiments only, so our children will have something to look forward to each week. Since our children may be rambunctious because they miss the exercise they'd normally get outdoors, we may think about coming up with an active educational game we can play inside the house, or we may consider making a punching bag, buying a trampoline, or borrowing a polka video from the library, anything that will get our children's excess energy out in a productive—or at least not destructive—manner.

As we've remarked before, homeschooling is what we make it. If we think homeschooling is boring and dreary, then our school year will be boring and dreary. Fortunately, it doesn't have to be. By taking a look at the liturgical calendar, we can find a favorite saint to celebrate each month and let our creativity run wild. We can make our celebration as spiritual or as educational or as fun as we want it to be. Sometimes we will emphasize one element, and at other times others. Sometimes, such as on St. Cecilia's Day, the patron of musicians, we may emphasize singing, while on the feast day of St. Francis de Sales, the patron of writers, we may emphasize memorizing poetry. On the feast day of St. Albert the Great, the patron of scientists, we may emphasize science experiments. Some years we may celebrate different saints as our family's needs and interests change. The main thing to remember is that we can bring joy to even the bleakest winter months with a little creativity, imagination, and faith.

# 43

## EMOTIONAL STRUGGLES

*"If you have a fearful thought, do not share it
with a weakling, whisper it to your saddle-bow
and ride forth singing."*

—KING ALFRED THE GREAT

MOTHERS are the heart of their families, and as such, we are responsible for the atmosphere in our homes. Our mood determines the mood of the household. As the old saying goes, "If Mama ain't happy, ain't nobody happy." Because our homeschooled children are home most, if not all, of the time, it is of the utmost importance to cultivate a cheerful, positive mindset to foster their emotional, intellectual, and spiritual development.

Since "out of the abundance of the heart the mouth speaketh" (Luke 6:45), we need first to carefully monitor our thoughts. We must heed St. Paul's injunction: "Whatsoever things are true, whatsoever modest, whatsoever just, whatsoever holy, whatsoever lovely, whatsoever of good fame, if there be any virtue, if any praise of discipline: think on these things" (Philippians 4:8). Therefore, we must develop the habit of thinking upbeat, positive thoughts about ourselves; self-disparagement is not a sign of humility but of a critical attitude that will, in turn, project itself onto others. With constant vigilance, we must examine every thought that comes into our mind before adopting it and embracing it as our own. Cultivating a positive mindset towards ourselves, our husband, children, home, and circumstances, will go far in generating a smiling face and cheerful words.

Likewise, we must monitor our speech. Let's try to avoid general negative statements like, "This always happens to me" or "This house is never neat" or "Nothing works around here!" Such statements give ourselves and our children a sense of futility and despair, a feeling that somehow everything is always wrong. We must also refrain from negative comments about ourselves and others (excluding, of course, the times when we make a conscious decision to correct a child, and then we do so with firmness and respect). Giving up negative speech is not easy and will take some time, and when we lose our temper, we may relapse into negative comments again. But we must not give up. Even if we don't succeed one hundred percent of the time, our home will be happier to the extent that we do succeed. Occasional slip-ups will have little effect once good habits are established. Perhaps the most effective way to build a habit of positive speech is to notice any time we say something negative, and then correct ourselves out loud: "Actually, most of the things in this house work very well. It's just difficult to wait until we can afford a new washing machine" or "I do a lot of things very well. I have many talents—and my dropping a carton of eggs is not a reflection on my overall ability as a wife and mother."

Of course, platitudes cannot cure depression or the moodiness caused by hormonal changes or by some trauma in our past. Some women find that herbs or Vitamin B supplements help decrease the mood swings caused by their menstrual cycle. Women with serious emotional issues may need to seek professional assistance, while others with milder problems may look for guidance in Christian self-help books. Often women must face and deal with issues of verbal, emotional, physical, or sexual abuse or other family dysfunctions from their past before they experience emotional healing. This can be painful and time-consuming, yet it is worth the investment of time, for our emotional healing will not only benefit us, but also our husband and children. Perhaps we can ask our husbands to listen as we try to verbally sort through our emotional issues, identify triggers, and work toward solutions. All of us come to a marriage with baggage of varying kinds and degrees, because no family upbringing is perfect, and we may really find remarkable improvement in our own happiness and in our marriage by examining the causes of our vulnerabilities. A good listener is crucial to this process; ideally our husband would be the best choice for this role. He may also find that he would benefit greatly by probing his own sensitivities and triggers while we listen patiently to him.

If we are struggling with moodiness or depression, we can pray to St. Dymphna, who was named patron saint of those with emotional problems because her own father wanted to marry her and killed her when she refused. She certainly understood the problems of a dysfunctional family! We can also turn to St. Elizabeth Seton, who suffered from depression as she struggled to raise her five children after her husband died. Because she converted to Catholicism shortly after her husband's death, many of her friends deserted her. Even after she started a school for her own children and others, which led to founding a new order of nuns, suffering continued to follow her as she watched two of her children die at young ages. She surely had heavy burdens to bear, but she offered her depression and grief to our crucified Lord. Widows or single mothers who home-school—or any of us struggling with emotional issues—may find solace in learning more about St. Elizabeth Seton and in imitating her courage through real hardship.

Psychological problems require psychological remedies, and we must seek the appropriate means to assist us in our difficulties. Nevertheless, spiritual aids can help us in our struggles by giving us the strength and hope to persevere. Creating a habit of positivity in our thoughts and our words will bring a measure of joy not just to us, but our entire household. When our emotions or moods begin to overwhelm us, we must turn our hearts to God, as a sunflower always turns towards the sun, and embrace our depression and other emotions as gifts from Him to help us grow in sanctity. While powerful emotions rage and storm in our hearts, we can keep our will united to His Will, our eyes fixed on Him. Most importantly, we must be sure to offer up our negative moods to Our Lord. Offering up our anger or depression may seem odd at first because we associate these negative emotions with our own sinfulness, but the emotion itself is not a sin, merely an occasion of sin, and only by surrendering even these negative feelings to God can we find the strength to deal with them and eventually overcome them. He does not despise any gift we offer Him, however strange; He is glad that we are turning our hearts to Him, even as we struggle through emotional typhoons. We do not understand why He sends us these trials, but we must not allow them to turn us away from Him. For God loves us, even when we do not love ourselves; God forgives us, even when we do not forgive ourselves; and God's merciful love is a vast ocean which can swallow up our faults and sinfulness without leaving a trace.

Our faith is a faith of joy and hope, a joy and hope that should permeate our hearts and our homes, even while we struggle with emotional issues. We live in a world where sin abounds, suffering exists, and death happens, but we believe in a God Whose mercy is infinite, Who promises resurrection from the dead and the joy of eternal life.

# 44

## GUILT

*"Gladly therefore will I glory in my
infirmities, that the power of Christ may
dwell in me. For which cause I please myself in
my infirmities, in reproaches, in necessities, in
persecutions, in distresses, for Christ. For when
I am weak, then am I powerful."*

—2 CORINTHIANS 12:9–10

HEALTHY guilt is a gift from God, reminding us of the evil we do when we sin; however, more and more today women are afflicted with an unhealthy guilt. Mothers seem to be particularly vulnerable to unhealthy guilt, possibly because of our great responsibility and our great love for our children. Every mistake we make or sin we commit has so much graver and longer-lasting consequences than before we became mothers! Often, abuse from our past—emotional, physical, or sexual—may make unhealthy guilt a frequent reaction, causing anger and depression. This is passed down in various forms to our children. Intellectually we may know that we have done nothing wrong in a given situation (or, if we have, that we are forgiven) but emotionally we can be overwhelmed with feelings of worthlessness, rage, or despair. Unexpected, trivial events may trigger these irrational guilty feelings. Seemingly innocuous contact with family members may elicit powerful emotional responses if our family was involved in this abuse, or if our family habitually criticizes us or our methods of raising and teaching our children.

All of this may sound more like psychology than spirituality, but the two are closely intertwined. Our emotional and psychological states profoundly affect our spiritual life, as well as our ability to be the wholesome, emotionally sound parents that we need to be to homeschool successfully. For those more seriously afflicted, sessions with a Christian counselor may prove invaluable. If unhealthy guilt, anger, or depression is damaging our spiritual life and our ability to love and teach our children, then we owe it to ourselves and to them to seek help. We must pray for the grace to find a counselor with the wisdom to address our particular difficulties.

While we struggle with our emotional trials, we must remember to distinguish between ourselves and our problems. We are not the problem. We have been burdened with a problem, and we may spend years heroically combating it—but though the problem may be imbedded in our psyche, it is distinct from ourselves. Furthermore, we must not expect immediate cure with no relapse. We have to accept our own imperfections, the imperfections of the past, of the present, and those that will show themselves in the future.

That is why the Christian life is so often called a battle—because the struggle against the weakness of our fallen human nature is not a one-time event, but a daily, ongoing war that ends only with death. St. Paul himself says, "And lest the greatness of the revelations should exalt me, there was given me a sting of my flesh, an angel of Satan, to buffet me. For which thing thrice I besought the Lord that it might depart from me. And he said to me: My grace is sufficient for thee; for power is made perfect in infirmity" (2 Corinthians 12: 7-9). Like St. Paul, we must realize that battling our weaknesses is our path to sanctity. This is how we can achieve holiness. Accepting our imperfections can be excruciatingly hard for people saddled with unhealthy guilt. But it also can be extraordinarily liberating. What did Mother Teresa say? "We are not called to be successful; we are called to be faithful." Being faithful doesn't mean we will never fail; it means we will get back up after every failure. We may not get back up on our feet every time; we may find ourselves crawling on our hands and knees, hanging on with broken fingernails. But isn't this, in itself, a type of martyrdom, a sort of heroism? Never to give up, no matter how hard or how far you fall; never to tire of humbly confessing our faults and resolving, once again, to do better; never to despair of the unseen ocean of God's mercy—this is the Christian life, and those who deny this have never striven for Christian perfection. Moreover, as our children see us struggling to overcome our emotional baggage, they can be inspired by the determination and perseverance we show. This memory may help them enormously in the future in their struggle against temptation or emotional trials of their own.

While we need to seek healing for our emotional wounds, we must also accept our emotions as our particular burden, one we must bear for Christ. They are an offering that only we can bring to His altar, begging that His grace and strength will be sufficient in our weakness.

# 45

## THE WEAKNESS OF THE SAINTS

*"Lord my God, Light of the blind,
and Strength of the weak; yea also
Light of those that see, and Strength of the
strong: hearken unto my soul, and hear it
crying out of the depths."*

—ST. AUGUSTINE

AS we have discussed already, St. Paul reveals briefly that he experienced some weakness, some thorn or sting, to remind him of his fallen human nature. However, St. Paul does not reveal what his tribulation was. Perhaps this is good, because it allows anyone to imagine that his own trial is similar to St. Paul's. It makes St. Paul's experience more universal. Yet sometimes specific examples can be encouraging to us. Knowing specific difficulties the saints have struggled with and overcome can inspire us to do persevere in our own struggles.

Unfortunately, the biographies of the saints often tend to gloss over the saints' human struggles and emphasize their almost superhuman penances and fasts, and their supernatural visions. Guilt-ridden sinners may be more discouraged than inspired by such biographies. Yet the saints were human and did struggle. We know that many saints were emotionally, physically, or sexually abused. Many experienced trauma, sometimes horrific trauma. While we may understand how they intellectually offered up such suffering, we have few glimpses into how they dealt with the all-too-human emotional reactions, such as resulting anger, guilt, depression, or fear, which are part of human nature's response to trauma.

Fortunately, there are exceptions. There are a few saints whose lives do reveal the same human emotions that characterize us all. One such saint is St. Thomas Aquinas. He is a wonderful model for homeschoolers for many reasons, first of all because he is the patron saint of students. At the age of five he was asking his teachers, "What is God?" In his teens he was locked up in a tower for nearly two years by his family, who opposed his vocation as a Dominican. He finally escaped and entered the Dominican Order in France, a safe distance from his belligerent family. (Let us not, then, feel guilty about separating ourselves from unhealthy influences, even close relatives.) Academically unsurpassed, he was so absorbed in theology that he spent a dinner at the king's table constructing an argument against the Manichean heresy. On the spiritual plain, he wrote the lyrics to some of the most moving hymns to the Holy Eucharist, including "Tantum Ergo" and "Adoro Te Devote." Nicknamed "the Dumb Ox," his robust figure did not recall the appearance of the typical ascetic. But apart from his comical absent-mindedness, his soaring intellect, and his even more sublime spirituality, St. Thomas is one of the few saints known to suffer from a phobia. As an infant, he and his sister shared a room until one night his sister was struck by lightening and died. After that, Thomas was terrified of lightening. Even when he was a Dominican priest, the sound of thunder would send him into the chapel where he would embrace the tabernacle until the end of the storm.

Let us take hope from our older brother in Christ in our own weakness. It is comforting to know that even the Angelic Doctor experienced the violence of human emotion and knew no remedy but Christ. Thus, when we kneel before Christ, bowed low with discouragement, heartache, and temptation to despair, bewildered and battered by the force of our own emotions, let us remember for a moment that spiritual giant, clinging desperately but trustingly to the Real Presence of Our Lord on earth.

# 46

## OUR SCHOOL OF LOVE

*"The school of Christ is the school of love.
In the last day, when the general examination
takes place, there will be no question at all
on the text of Aristotle, the aphorisms of
Hippocrates, or the Paragraphs of Justinian.
Love will be the whole syllabus."*

—ST. ROBERT BELLARMINE

WE have many goals in mind while engaged in raising and educating our children. We want them to master the basics of reading, writing, mathematics, science, history, geography, a foreign language, music, and art. We want them to learn basic cooking, mending, and computer skills and to cultivate healthy habits regarding food and exercise. We want them to grow up to be well-read, articulate, courteous, responsible, self-supporting, confident, cultured, happy, and law-abiding citizens who employ their skills to contribute to their community. We want our children to find a career and a vocation that will enable them to use their talents and that will bring them joy and fulfillment. Yet our primary and most important goal for our children is even greater than all these things: we want them to become holy—to be saints.

Sanctity is not meant only for nuns or priests or the few canonized heroes and heroines of our faith; sanctity is to be lived by all, throughout the trivial ups and downs of our mostly uneventful lives. Properly speaking, everyone in heaven is a saint; their souls were purified either by acts of virtue and self-sacrifice here on earth or by the cleansing fires of Purgatory. Therefore, to fail to be a saint is to be doomed to hell. Holiness is what we were made for; holiness alone brings complete fulfillment and joy, for holiness is simply growing closer to, and more like, God, Who is our Beginning and our End, and in Whom alone we find our happiness and our peace.

Moreover, sanctity is not meant only for adults; adults are what they are in a great measure because of their formation as children and because of the habits they developed during childhood. Furthermore, history has shown us the impact that holy children can make. St. Therese of Lisieux's prayers as a child converted a hardened criminal on his way to execution. Blessed Jacinta and Francesco, two of the three seers at Fatima, have inspired millions by their lives of prayer and sacrifice, though both died before they reached their teens. St. Dominic Savio, St. Maria Goretti, St. Germaine, St. Aloysius Gonzaga, St. Agnes, St. Stanislaus Kostka, St. Tarcisius, and many more have shown to the world what heights of holiness the young have reached. We must take seriously, then, our obligation to foster holiness in our children.

What are the best means to mold saints? We have already discussed many of them in our chapter on nurturing priestly and religious vocations, for all holy men and women, whether priests, monks, nuns, husbands, wives, or single, need to develop the same virtues and habits that lead to sanctity. Devotion to the saints, daily prayer and spiritual reading, frequent confession and communion, regular visits to the Blessed Sacrament, celebration of the many liturgical seasons throughout the year—all of these will encourage not only religious or priestly vocations, but the sanctity that is needed in all walks of life.

What will speak more powerfully to our children than anything else, however, is our own example. Do we honestly believe, as Leon Bloy once said, that "there is only one sorrow, the sorrow of not being a saint"? Do our lives reflect this conviction so strongly that our children can sense it? If we really believe that the only sorrow is not to become a saint, then we must work to become saints. We must spend time with Christ in prayer and spiritual reading. We must become like Christ and mirror Christ to our children; they must meet Christ in us, with His gentleness, mercy, wisdom, justice, authority, forgiveness. They must feel Christ's love in our love for them.

For what is sanctity but love of God? And how will our children learn to love God except by seeing us love God both in Himself and in others? We need to teach our children to love, and the best way is to love them: to correct their faults gently, to bear their mistakes patiently, to care for their needs cheerfully, to discipline them calmly and firmly, to listen to them attentively, to speak to them kindly and wisely, and to pray with them reverently. If they see Christ's love shining through us in these ways, then they will fall in love with Him, and that is the whole secret of holiness.

Thus our homeschool becomes a school of love. Many subjects are studied here—but while studying each subject, our children also learn love. Eventually, they learn that everything they do, whether playing, singing, scrubbing, raking, adding, subtracting, reading, or writing, can be an act of love. Each action is a tiny but meaningful response from us to the infinite ocean of love God showers on us. Our children learn to find love in everything, from tying their little brother's shoes to building a snowman. In every little event in life, they see God's love for them, and in everything they offer back to Him their love. Times of sorrow or suffering are thereby transformed into joys, and times of rejoicing are lifted to gloriously supernatural heights.

If our homeschool includes occasional visits to a local church or adoration chapel, our children will encounter Christ's love for them face to face. Mother Teresa once said, "When you look at the crucifix, you understand how much Jesus loved you then. When you look at the Sacred Host you understand how much Jesus loves you now." How true this insight is! In the Holy Eucharist, our children will find the most concrete, practical proof of our

Savior's love for each of them, right here and now. He does not reign only in heaven on a remote, lofty throne; rather, desiring to reign in our hearts as well, He imprisons Himself in the tabernacle or monstrance, waiting for us to visit Him—and at Mass He deigns to actually enter into our hearts to complete His conquest.

What tremendous love He bears us! For He does not merely consent to come to us—no, He ardently longs for this most intimate union: "With desire I have desired to eat this pasch with you" (Luke 22:15). The Blessed Sacrament is not man's invention that Christ thought over and approved; no mere creature ever could have dared to dream up such wondrous condescension! No, Our Lord Himself instituted this sacrament because "My delights were to be with the children of men" (Proverbs 8:31). How can we not respond to such love? How can we remain so cold and indifferent, or even so tepid and weak, when we experience the furious, passionate outpouring Christ's love in this sacrament?

The goal of our homeschool is to show our children this stupendous, incomprehensible love that God bears them, and to cultivate in them a responsive love—a love of God that will motivate and animate all of their thoughts, words, and deeds, finding fruition in prayer, self-sacrifice, and acts of love for others.

St. John tells us, "God is love" (1 John 4:8). Let our homeschool be permeated with God's love for us and our love for Him, until it is truly a school of love.

# PRAYERS FOR HOMESCHOOLERS

## PRAYER OF A HOMESCHOOLER

*"It is simply impossible to lead, without
the aid of payer, a virtuous life."*
—ST. JOHN CHRYSOSTOM

ETERNAL Father, I thank Thee for blessing me with the children Thou hast given me, and for granting me the opportunity of homeschooling them. Help me to provide them with an atmosphere of love, peace, purity, self-sacrifice, and joy so that they may develop the virtues they need to lead holy, Christian lives. May they learn all they need to know in all their subjects, but especially may they learn to love Thee and to show this love for Thee through acts of love for others. May I do my part to fill their spiritual, emotional, physical, and intellectual needs, and model to them Thine own patient and forgiving love. May our homeschool turn into a true school of love, where our family learns to love Thee in everything that happens to us, and in everyone that we see, so that someday our family may meet again in heaven, where we will see face-to-face, Thou, Who art Love. Amen.

# PRAYER IN TIME OF DIFFICULTIES

*"Prayer is the best weapon we possess, the key that opens the heart of God."*

—ST. PIO

DEAREST Lord, please come to my aid in this, my hour of need! Thou hast given me this child; do not withhold the graces I need to raise and educate him. Teach me to understand his needs, allow me to understand the reason why I am experiencing this difficulty in raising him, and help me to assist him in exactly the way that will benefit him most. Merciful Lord, may my child see in my eyes, in my words, and in my actions, the maternal love I bear him; even more, may my child see in me a reflection of that infinite love that Thou bearest for him. Help me to put aside the worry and anxiety I feel for him right now and to relax with him and treasure each moment I have with him at this age.

Dear Lord, have mercy on a mother's pleas and grant me the wisdom, the prudence, and the courage to recognize and overcome the challenges that face me, and grant me the patience and love to deal with the difficulties until they are resolved. I ask this with confidence, O Lord, for I know Thou wilt grant me the graces I need to fulfill my duties as a mother. Lord, have mercy on me! Amen.

# PRAYER OF A NEW HOMESCHOOLER

*"Christian wife! Follow in the footsteps of the ideal of all womanhood, the Blessed Mother of God; in joy and in sorrow, she will be your advocate at the throne of her Son."*

—ST. JOHN VIANNEY

O Blessed Mother, what fear, yet what anticipation, fills my heart at this moment! What a wonderful, exciting opportunity to raise and form my children according to true Christian ideals; yet how frighteningly tremendous is the task that faces me! I long for the chance to spend these precious moments with my children, yet I doubt my own ability—my ability to be sufficiently patient, organized, knowledgeable, and wise to succeed at running a household and educating my children. Be with me every day, dearest Mother. Help me to keep my heart turned to Our Lord in every circumstance; fill my mind with thy wisdom, Our Lady of Good Counsel; fill my heart with thy patience, O Refuge of Sinners!

Thank thy Divine Son for me for granting me this great privilege of teaching my children, and ask Him to grant me the grace and strength to raise my children to be well-educated, virtuous, and faithful Catholics. May I impart to them a true faith in Him and a deep love for His holy Church and for all the sacraments, especially for the Holy Eucharist. I love thee, O Blessed Mother! Do not desert me in this great endeavor, but be at my side every moment and help me to foster in my children a love of learning, a love of reading, and especially a love for thee and for thy Divine Son. Instill in my family a great devotion for the rosary, that by this garland of prayers, we may draw closer to each other and closer to thy Divine Son by meditating on His life and by honoring thee, His Mother. Pray for me, Sweet Advocate, and pray for my children. Amen.

# PRAYER TO ST. THOMAS AQUINAS

*"Perfect married life means the complete dedication of the parents for the benefit of the children."*

—ST. THOMAS AQUINAS

O Angelic Doctor, St. Thomas Aquinas, who attained great heights of wisdom and knowledge during your

time on earth, help me to homeschool my children. Help me
to foster in them the same curiosity and eagerness to learn
as you showed when you asked at age five, "What is God?"
Help them to learn all that they need to know to succeed in
this life, but to realize, like you, that they will learn the most
valuable lessons at the foot of the crucifix. May my children
prize above all else the wisdom and love of Our Lord. Pray
for me, that as their mother and teacher, I may lead them
patiently and lovingly towards Him Who is Truth. Pray for
them, that they may not be harmed by my faults and that
they may be open and receptive to the true wisdom. Amen.

# PRAYER TO ST. ELIZABETH ANN SETON

*"We must pray literally without ceasing—
without ceasing; in every occurrence and
employment of our lives. You know I mean
that prayer of the heart which is independent
of place or situation, or which is, rather, a
habit of lifting up the heart to God, as in a
constant communication with Him."*

—ST. ELIZABETH ANN SETON

ST. Elizabeth Ann Seton, you knew the difficulties and
anxieties of raising and educating your children. Help

me now to raise and educate my children to be cultured, well-read, and knowledgeable citizens of our society, and even more, eventually, holy and virtuous citizens of heaven. My life, like yours, is full of many cares and responsibilities. May I not be weighed down by my burdens, but place them trustfully in the hands of Christ. Help me to frequently lift my heart to our dear Lord in prayer, and being close to Him, help my children to draw close to Him as well. Amen.

# ABOUT THE AUTHOR

AGNES M. PENNY, the youngest of twelve children, was born and grew up in Norwood, Massachusetts. She attended Christendom College in Front Royal, Virginia, where she met her future husband, Daniel. She graduated in 1997 with a degree in English Literature and married the following year. She is the mother of nine children, whom she enjoys homeschooling, and the author of two other books on motherhood, *Your Labor of Love* and *Your Vocation of Love*. She has also written articles for various periodicals, including *The National Catholic Register, The New Oxford Review, Back Home Magazine, Home Education Magazine* and *mater et magistra*. She lives with her family in Whitehall, Pennsylvania.

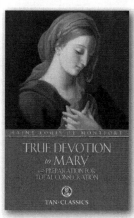

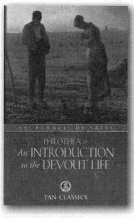

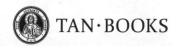

978-0-89555-153-5

978-0-89555-149-8

978-0-89555-199-3

The collection includes distinguished spiritual works of the saints, philosophical treatises and famous biographies.

978-0-89555-226-6

978-0-89555-152-8

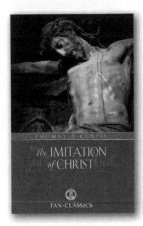

978-0-89555-225-9

Visit us at TANBooks.com

# TAN·BOOKS

TAN Books was founded in 1967 to preserve the spiritual, intellectual and liturgical traditions of the Catholic Church. At a critical moment in history TAN kept alive the great classics of the Faith and drew many to the Church. In 2008 TAN was acquired by Saint Benedict Press. Today TAN continues its mission to a new generation of readers.

From its earliest days TAN has published a range of booklets that teach and defend the Faith. Through partnerships with organizations, apostolates, and mission-minded individuals, well over 10 million TAN booklets have been distributed.

More recently, TAN has expanded its publishing with the launch of Catholic calendars and daily planners—as well as Bibles, fiction, and multimedia products through its sister imprints Catholic Courses (CatholicCourses.com) and Saint Benedict Press (SaintBenedictPress.com).

Today TAN publishes over 500 titles in the areas of theology, prayer, devotions, doctrine, Church history, and the lives of the saints. TAN books are published in multiple languages and found throughout the world in schools, parishes, bookstores and homes.

For a free catalog, visit us online at
**TANBooks.com**

Or call us toll-free at
**(800) 437-5876**